From Mindless to Mindful

From Mindless to Mindful

How to Create Memorable Service Experiences

Draj Fozard and Jesse Otta

INSOMNIAC PRESS

Cover design by Mike O'Connor. Cover image by iStockphoto.com.

Library and Archives Canada Cataloguing in Publication

Fozard, Draj, 1956-, author
From mindless to mindful / Draj Fozard, Jesse Otta.

ISBN 978-1-55483-139-5 (pbk.)

1. Customer services. I. Otta, Jesse, 1986-, author
II. Title.

HF5415.5.F69 2014   658.8'12   C2014-907352-6

The publisher gratefully acknowledges the support of the Department
of Canadian Heritage through the Canada Book Fund.

Printed and bound in Canada

Insomniac Press, 520 Princess Ave.
London, Ontario, Canada, N6B 2B8
www.insomniacpress.com

To my sons, Michael and Nicholas
Love you more
—Draj

To my grandparents, who set the foundation;
to my parents, who built the house;
and to Draj, who opened the door.

Thank you
—Jesse

"The years teach much which the days never know."

— Ralph Waldo Emerson, "Experience"

Contents

Foreword

This book provides a fresh perspective on the value of customer service and how to implement a program that produces results. The authors offer two unique perspectives from two different vantage points that merge into their overall theme.

I think any employee wishing to enhance their service ability and every manager wanting to provide a differentiated level of service will find value in this book. There are countless books on service, but the way these stories deliver their messages will resonate with you.

Customers return when they receive value, and customers give referrals when they receive value. Price is one value, but, as we all know, we don't buy simply on price. Our loyalty is enhanced when our service experience exceeds our expectations. The stories in this book bring to life the excitement and personal rewards of being of real service to people.

Any business wanting to prosper needs to heed the messages in this book. Any employee wanting to be a manager needs to heed the messages in this book. Any manager wanting to be truly successful needs to heed the messages in this book.

Gary L. Ford
Author of *Life Is Sales* and *Life Is Management*

Chapter 1

From Mindless to Mindful

"How the hell did we end up here?"

This was the question a former bank executive posed to her relatively new recruit. Her recruit, a kid who came from a car wash, felt as if he should be the one asking the question. It was only ten years ago when he started washing cars in a small town. That was a far cry from where he was sitting. He was now on the iconic stage of business and economics in the financial heart of Canada: Bay Street. Without hesitation, he shot back to her, "I don't have the slightest clue, but it sure has been an interesting journey. Wouldn't you agree?" She nodded in agreement as he turned to gaze out the window. They sat in the branch of the credit union for which they both worked while Bay Street bankers and busy-looking movers and shakers darted up and down the bustling street outside. Inside the quiet office, the two watched and reflected on their respective journeys.

The real question was, "What were *they* doing there?" The busy businesspeople outside wore a mix of perfectly tailored suits, both classic and trendy, and outfits that were hardly the cold, soggy boots and wet pants commonly found in a car wash. At a glance, it appeared that the young man was from the other side of the tracks, out of his element. On the other hand, the former bank executive seemed as if she were a better fit in this setting. With her classic Cartier watch ticking in symphony with the jingling of her Tiffany bracelets, she could have easily strolled out into the street, looking sharp and playing the part. Even though she was more familiar on this stage, the reason she was in the branch that day was making her nervous.

So what *were* they doing there?

The unlikely duo were moments away from launching the pilot of their new customer service program that was a distillation of all they had learned over their vastly different careers. The goal of their program was to inspire memorable customer service. They had discovered through shared stories and conversations that, regardless of their generational gap and careers in unique industries, the same basic principles of delivering memorable customer service experiences applied. From the first few days of working together they knew they needed to tie their experiences together somehow and create something, but what would that look like?

They went guerrilla—this unlikely duo, "the Banker" and "the Kid"— and decided to create a program based on their personal experiences and research, and they envisioned a program that would teach and inspire others. It was positioned as a program that would greatly improve the already highly regarded service of the credit union. This was a lofty goal, and no matter how much they believed in their program, it still made them nervous. What if it turned out to be a disaster? What if no one took their homegrown ideas and stories seriously? After all, this was their creation, their brainchild. Perhaps no one would share their excitement.

They had a lot riding on this. The Banker's reputation was on the line, and this was the Kid's big chance to prove himself in a new industry. So what would they have to do to make sure the pilot for their program was a success?

Hearts and Minds

The program's success was only achievable by capturing the hearts and minds of the staff in the pilot branches.

The pilot program drew from the stories and the people that inspired both the Banker and the Kid throughout their individual careers. They happen to be the same stories and people that you will get to know in this book. Today, organizations face distractions that create barriers to memorable customer service. Customer service focused processes, while well intentioned, may cause the customer experience to fall flat in today's invariably dynamic and hyperstimulating marketplace.

Mindlessness, as referenced in this book, is about the absence of consideration of certain aspects of the customer experience. One can still be satisfied with a mindlessly delivered service, but chances are that it won't be memorable. You have probably experienced this yourself when buying groceries. How many times have you heard the scripted line "Did you find everything you were looking for?" It is a well-intentioned question and likely part of a defined customer interaction process. But when it's asked robotically and without sincerity or eye contact, in the back of your mind you may be thinking, "Do you *really* care?" Organizations need to move beyond a one-size-fits-all approach and find ways to inspire memorable customer experiences.

The Banker and the Kid have themselves moved from mindless to mindful by filtering out all the noise, and they invite you to join them as they remember the stories of what happened along the way.

By now you might be asking yourself whether this is just yet another customer service book. Is this one of the thousands of books on Amazon claiming to have the perfect program for promoting outstanding customer service and improving the bottom line? Yeah, those books, the ones full of studies, stats, quadrant analyses, and customer interaction cycles. You know, the books with creative acronyms to remind employees about how to talk and how to walk, the how-tos and the what-not-to-dos.

Nope. Sorry. This is not one of *those* books.

This book offers no promises, just reminders. It's a simple book about customer service based on common truths. It demonstrates these truths as revealed along two different paths. It shows how those paths eventually crossed against many odds. It will take you on a journey—a journey to remind you of what truly matters when striving to create personal and memorable customer experiences. It might even make you laugh a few times!

In the following chapters, you will read about the real people whose stories demonstrate the important truths and reminders of mindful customer service. They are all fascinating individuals in their own right, but more important, they each have interesting stories to tell. Each has shaped and contributed to many lives with positivity, style, and grace. All have discovered their own individual secrets to establishing personal and memorable connections. It is through their eyes and their stories that you will be able to take the lessons and mindfully apply them to your daily life—at work and at home.

So, about the Banker's original question to the Kid…. How the hell *did* they end up in that branch on the eve of their customer service pilot program?

Chapter 2

The Banker and the Kid

The Banker

I have often wondered how I ended up spending my entire working life in the financial services sector. It was not how I thought my life would turn out, but then again, whose life really does?

My first recollection of a bank comes from the trips my father and I would take every Thursday to the TD Bank in downtown Sudbury. Sudbury is where I grew up—cold winters, the Big Nickel, and salt-of-the-earth folk. You have probably at least heard a bit about the place from the late Stompin' Tom Connors. Our trip to the bank was a weekly jaunt. Sometimes we walked, but usually we took the bus into town. Afterwards we would cross the street and go to Kresge's for a pop and French fries. What a treat!

The bank was a huge, cavernous marble building, seemingly that much bigger through the eyes of a child. We would line up behind the other people, where we would wait, shuffle a few steps, and then wait again. All of this waiting would make me very curious about this place, and by the time it was our turn at the counter, I would be ready to explore and explode. My father always had other plans, and he would swiftly swoop me up with one arm and place me on the counter, keeping me safely in his line of sight. It was all quite the mystery to me, as the woman behind the counter would take my father's cheque, look at the cheque, then look at my father, then look at the cheque again. She would then ask him to sign it, after which she would stare at his signature, stare at him again, and then loudly stamp the cheque with a *thump!* After this strange routine, she would finally reach into a magic drawer that was always full of money! She would then count the money. Three times! Twice to herself and once to my father, who barely spoke English. It was like this every time, and I remember wondering why the woman behind the counter never smiled back, but, boy, could she ever count money fast!

One week near Christmas, my father lined up in front of a different teller. She looked up and asked my father how he pronounced his name. That had never happened before. After she cashed his cheque, she did something else that was new in our Thursday routine. She asked my father one more question, and it excited me. She asked him if she could give me a candy cane! A candy cane? At a *bank*? I cracked a shy grin, and when she smiled at me, it was a done deal. I liked her. This new teller, Ms. Susan, became my favourite person at the bank, and each time we visited, I would gently tug at my father to stand in her line, even though it was always the longest. Ms. Susan had the most beautiful smile, she looked happy, and she made my father and me feel special despite the language barrier.

My parents were just in their early twenties when they arrived in Canada with me in tow. The story I've been told is that after the Second World War, my maternal grandfather, who had been a POW in a German camp, knowing he couldn't go back to the former Yugoslavia, had a choice between Canada or Australia to emigrate to. That one decision, perhaps made with a flip of a coin, profoundly altered the course of many lives. My father, who was orphaned during the war at the age of nine, left his siblings, and in May 1958, he, my mother, and I boarded a train bound for France to begin a long voyage across the ocean. It was a voyage that would take us to a strange new country and a different future.

Carried by the good ship *Ivernia*, my parents were excited and scared at the same time, wondering if they had made the right decision to join my grandparents in Canada. It was a long voyage, and my parents got seasick, while I felt nothing but curiosity and wonder. My parents have described many a time how their little, blonde-haired tot charmed all on board and gave them a sense of comfort that their decision was the right one to make. How brave they were to choose to leave all that was familiar, to leave the only home they knew and begin a new life in Canada.

Being that I was the daughter of first-generation

immigrants, my education became the priority in my family. Growing up, I knew that my parents' expectations of me were extremely high. I needed to get excellent marks so I could, as they would say, make something of my life. My mother wanted me to be a pharmacist, and my father thought being a teacher would be good job. I had set my sights on going to law school, knowing that I had to end up being some sort of professional. I just didn't know exactly what. I was left to forge my own way with basically no one to provide academic or career guidance. I traded those cold winters in Sudbury for Hamilton, Ontario, and McMaster University, where I enrolled in a first-year general arts program. I was confident that the world was my oyster and the future was mine to create.

I was in the midst of creating my ideal future, strategically working at the Family Court Division back home in Sudbury during the summer before my final year of university. Mrs. T., a graceful older lady, was the court reporter, and she had taken a motherly liking to me as I recall—always listening and providing advice. That summer, she gave me a parting gift, $20 and a card to help me on my way. She also told me she would put in a good word with her son in case I wanted a job once I graduated. Her son turned out to be the vice president of human resources at a trust company. Seeing a great opportunity, I decided to shelve my application to law school and decline the offer I received to attend teachers college, and I let life grab me gently by the wrist. In

January 1979, I became a management trainee at Canada Trust, and there, after completing my degree, I began the best education I could ever ask for.

Up to that point, my concept of service in a financial institution was basically rooted in transactional elements such as efficiency and accuracy: get 'em in, get 'em out, and *don't* make a mistake. Tellers were evaluated on how quickly they got rid of the line and how long it took to balance their cash at the end of the day. In those early days, I also observed an unwritten rule: Don't ask customers too many questions; you don't want to appear too nosey. Heaven forbid you ask what a new account was for or ask about the origins of a large cash deposit. (Oh, how things would change post-9/11.)

In 1979, banking was still mostly paper-based, and computers were just being introduced. Banks, for the most part, didn't consider themselves retail stores, and they certainly didn't, in my opinion, put customers at the centre of their strategic and operational plans. They were in the business of making money and answering to their shareholders—not so much their customers. Day-to-day business was conducted on their terms and their requirements. Hours of operation were typically convenient for the bankers, and their customers had to live with that.

I didn't know it then, but my new employer, that little trust company from London, Ontario, was going to change all that and take me along for the ride. Canada Trust's retail focus and strategy was just beginning. They were going to make Canada's "Big Five" banks—RBC, TD, Scotiabank, BMO, and CIBC—sit up and take notice. Canada Trust was embarking on their journey to revolutionize the customer service banking experience—all facets of it. This would even include changing an industry norm that was the ire of the general population: banking hours. Instead of the traditional 9:00 a.m. to 3:00 p.m. on Monday to Friday, we were open "from 8 to 8" and six days straight. Yes, even Saturdays. "Banking hours" had become "customer hours," and as progressive as that was for those times, it was only the beginning.

For the next twenty-three years, I was fortunate enough to grow my career in an organization that was purposeful and strategic in all things that focused on customers. The service experience was entrenched in heart of the organization's culture, and all levels of the organization held themselves accountable. Creativity and innovation were embraced, and Canada Trust changed the competitive landscape of retail banking in Canada. In 2000, TD Bank acquired Canada Trust. TD was very interested in the innovative service culture that Canada Trust had built. Their investment has paid off, as today the organization is highly regarded for its customer service, has seen unprecedented growth, and is one of the most successful banks in North America.

It was a privilege and honour to work there. As my career ascended, I learned so much every step of the way. The experience and education I gained truly helped me fulfill my parents' wishes for me to make something of my life. More important, the insights and wisdom I've collected have made me mindful of what really matters and, thankfully, what doesn't.

The Banker Meets the Kid

It was February 14, 2013, and I remember standing in front of the mirror that morning, thinking, "I'm going to lose my mind." No, not because there wouldn't be a dozen long-stem red roses on Valentine's Day (yet again), and not because it was the middle of winter and I hate the cold. My self-diagnosis was due to the current state of my job. You see, I was six weeks into a new position and finding myself challenged. As the director of service of a major Canadian credit union, a key responsibility of mine was to deal with customer inquiries and/or complaints that escalated beyond a branch or regional level. Although I had over twenty-five years of frontline customer relations experience, none of these complaints could be resolved by a one-size-fits-all solution. While the volume of complaints was relatively low, each one required time-consuming individual attention and commitment.

I was very busy with more on my plate than any person's appetite could handle! Aside from acting in the capacity of ombudsperson, my other responsibilities included acting as relationship manager for our customer experience program, director for our members' telephone banking contact centre, deputy privacy officer, and delivery lead for corporate projects. Given this exhaustive list, it came as no surprise to my vice president when I politely let him know that the "best version of myself" was not happening, and it was certainly not going to happen with the current volume of work. (The wailing from my corner cubicle surely must have supported my cause.) Being the wise leader that he is, my vice president readily approved the addition of a customer experience coordinator to assist me. Enter Jesse Otta, a kid from a car wash.

Jesse was one of nine candidates I interviewed for this junior position. He made it to a shortlist of three. Everyone on this final flight was worthy of getting the job, and any one of them would have been a great addition to the team. Intelligent and driven, they all brought something different to the table. I knew I was going to have a difficult time making my decision. In true fashion, I wanted it all. They had to possess superior customer service skills and be able to solve problems on their own, but those were givens. I was also looking for positivity, a sense of humour, and enthusiasm. The words of Ralph Waldo Emerson resonated in my mind: "Nothing great was ever achieved without enthusiasm." I was planning to accomplish great things in this new role of mine, and I needed a co-pilot who wanted to, in addition to being able to, fly the plane while we were still building it and to do so with warmth and enthusiasm.

It was his smile. Yes, I think that's what I noticed

first. One couldn't help but smile right back. Right from our very first interview to the final fourth coffee at Starbucks, he shared his stories about his past work experiences at the car wash with boundless positivity and enthusiasm. I must have asked him the same question six different ways, and he didn't miss a beat. There was a certain confidence to his answers, and yet a quiet humility in his responses. He sounded like he had also learned a few life lessons along the way.

Sitting across from him then and listening to him talk, I remember the little voice in my head saying, "To be so passionate about running a car wash of all places.... What's up with that?" Perhaps it was our age difference, perhaps it was our different experiences, but either way, I could not quite understand his excitement about washing cars and some of the characters he told me about. I also wondered just how his background was going to assist him in dealing with issues I felt were a bit more complex than what he was used to. Fortunately, I have learned in my working life that when passion is partnered with positivity and enthusiasm, it will move mountains. In Jesse's case, cars and soapsuds too!

Jesse got the job. And little did I know that I would discover the answers to all my questions and so much more in the months following that final coffee at Starbucks on a sunny spring day.

I once read somewhere that when the student is ready, the teacher appears. It didn't take long for Jesse and me to recognize that we truly shared a passion for finding ways to deliver a "personal and different" service experience. The bigger surprise was finding the roles of student and teacher becoming interchangeable as we increasingly looked to each other for support and guidance. The overwhelming complexity of some of the issues we dealt with demanded thoughtful discussion and analysis. Experience has taught me to seek help, get another perspective, listen, and suspend judgement. We were about to develop our service program, and we would meet daily to complete some of the early stage planning. I believe it was during one of these sessions that the idea of a book started to form in my mind. We had such great ideas and stories, and I thought about how exciting it would be to capture it all and share it with others! But I was hesitant to say anything, as it was less than six months since we started working together. I was sure he would think of me as delusional.

A book. How in the world would I ever present this idea?

The "how" came in the form of a workshop that we both attended in early fall of 2013. It was a seminar put on by the exceptional DeGroote School of Business featuring the wonderful folks at Disney detailing their approach to quality service. Midway through the morning, however, the management of White Oaks Resort & Spa, the facility that was hosting the workshop, needed to make an announcement. The unthinkable had happened. Construction activities in the vicinity had severed a major water line, and the resort no longer had running water. Seriously, an upscale 220-unit resort had their water shut off without warning. A nightmare situation. No washing dishes, running showers, or flushing toilets. Now that, to me, was an Emergency (yes, with a capital *E*).

As the management prepared to make their announcement to the hundreds of attendees in the ballroom, I was thinking, "This isn't going to be easy. Jeez…. I'm glad I'm not in *their* shoes." Jesse and I looked at each other. We were both wondering how they were going to figure this one out. But figure it out they did. What happened next, and, more important, how it was handled, exemplified grace under pressure. The sky would not fall on this day—storm clouds, and maybe a few drops, but no deluge.

The management communicated immediately with clarity and sincerity. We may not have had water, but at least we weren't left in the dark! They let us know what had caused the problem and what they were going to do about it. We expected to wait until the city had fixed the water main, but White Oaks had other ideas. The management had ordered water tankers to deliver fresh water in the meantime. We knew water was on the way, and although the problem wasn't caused by White Oaks, they took responsibility to provide a temporary solution. Their guests came first. I feel fortunate to have watched the event unfold before my eyes. I literally had a front-row seat. With admiration, I witnessed a fine demonstration of putting customers first that happened to be against the backdrop of a Disney quality service workshop.

I was impressed, and I thought that this would make a great story to tell. A story for a book? A spark had been lit. This created the opportunity I needed to pitch my book idea to Jesse. I knew we both had this mad desire to share our stories, to demonstrate what we learned to be true about customer service, and to create something special together.

Though I hate having my picture taken, on this day, I was excited enough to acquiesce to Jesse's photo request. As we stood in front of some colourful balloons emblazoned with mouse ears, I whispered to him, "We should write a book." With smiles on our faces almost as big as the line of water trucks outside, the camera clicked. The wheels had been set into motion. Our story had begun.

The Kid

Car Wash 101

I may have felt nervous heading into my very first job interview, but I was confident that I knew what I had to do to succeed. I donned a crisp, new shirt, and it hung from my thin fourteen-year-old frame as if it were still on the hanger. I had a backup resume on hand in case Claudio, the car wash owner who was to interview me, had misplaced the original copy. For a week straight,

I had practiced mock interviews with my seventeen-year-old brother, Joey, who, to me, was an expert senior human resources consultant. I pored over my resume in fine detail. My oldest brother, Mike, and I practiced the difficult questions I may be faced with during what I imagined would be the interview of my young life. Though my parents preferred I wait another year or two before entering the workforce, I had a very real and personal reason to find a job. I wanted to save up enough money to buy a new moped.

My mother fired up our GMC Safari as I jumped in the passenger seat. Little did I know that the short trip to the car wash was only the beginning of a much longer journey. As my mother reluctantly piloted our family van towards the car wash, my imaginative young mind was in overdrive. Envisioning scenarios where I dazzled Claudio with my compelling and well-thought-out answers to his questions. I was an A student with a nicely formatted resume and interesting hobbies. How could he be anything short of impressed?

We pulled into the parking lot of the adjacent market.

"Well, good luck," said my loving mother. "Smile, and don't be nervous. Just be yourself—nobody is better at that than you."

Without looking at her, I hopped out of the van and replied, "Luck is for losers. Don't worry. I know exactly what I'm doing."

My smug remark didn't frustrate her. Instead, my biggest fan smiled knowingly to herself. Her overconfident teenaged son would soon discover otherwise.

I walked towards the car wash office with teenaged swagger, oozing confidence akin to a heavyweight boxing champion of the world. I was Muhammad Ali, and this job interview was George Foreman—*rumble, young man, rumble!* Just beyond the office door stood a man of average height. He had a muscular build and could have been cast in a movie as a stereotypical bodyguard. I opened the door and stepped inside, catching his attention and causing him to turn towards me.

"Hello, I'm Jesse," I said to him as I politely passed him a copy of my resume. "I'm here to see Claudio for an interview."

I respectfully extended my hand towards him, and as we shook hands for the first time, he replied, "Hi, I'm Claudio. Can you work?"

Thinking he was asking about my competency, I blurted out, "Of course!"

What happened next shocked me. Claudio abruptly ended my first job interview. He gave me the job and said, "Okay then. Do you see the guy standing across from us folding towels? His name is Tim, and he will show you what to do."

As I walked towards Tim, I glanced back to see Claudio toss my prized resume into a car wash pail repurposed as a trash can. All of the exhaustive preparation was for nothing.

My mother was right, and I was wrong. Do you know how I got my first job that day? Luck. On that day, the weather had improved from cloudy and bleak to bright and sunny, leaving Claudio short staffed with three hours left until closing time. He needed extra help, and I appeared at the right place at the right time. I learned a good lesson about listening that day. I'm sorry, Mom, and thanks for wishing me luck—it worked. Contrary to my mindset earlier that day, I had come to the realization that I wasn't the heavyweight I imagined myself to be.

Despite this, my first day on the job wasn't a total knockout punch. I would begin to learn the ropes, as I set out to master the fine art of washing, drying, and folding towels in addition to drying off cars, performing final quality assurance checks, and, most important, interacting with our customers. I remembered what my father had told me in preparation for job interviews and entering the working world: "Never stop working, even if there is nothing to do. Find something to do, and if you can't find something, then ask how you can help." I focused on this and my mother's advice before the interview: smile. Flashing a big grin full of shiny metal braces while asking customers how else I could help them ended up paying off more than you'd think. After my new team and I had completed our end-of-the-day cleanup duties, Claudio split up the money collected in the daily tip jar. I received my piece of the pie for my first three-hour shift: one single dollar.

I still treasure that dollar coin to this day as a reminder of a lesson learned. Receiving that one-dollar tip was the beginning of my realization of the importance of a great customer experience. I realized that providing better experiences meant receiving more tips. I smiled and smiled. My moped awaited, and I couldn't earn those tips fast enough. Delighting our customers not only meant more tips, it also made the days in a tough job easier in my finding new ways to make others smile.

My passion was born that first day in the car wash, and my journey continued over the next ten years. It was a journey filled with bright-eyed wonder and an enthusiasm to learn as much as I could about improving customer experiences from the extraordinary people I interacted with.

Me? The Manager?

When you grow up in a lakeside port village, there is an undeniable air of excitement during the summertime. I know this all too well. As the harsh Canadian winter fades away, heavy coats and boots are swapped with board shorts and flip flops, and typically responsible twenty-one-year-olds become much less typical.

The entry to my twenty-first summer followed my exit from university. Compared to most people's departure from formal post-secondary education, mine was much less distinguished. I was suspended, and while I should have cared, I didn't. There was no need to attend a graduation ceremony. I had no cap to toss into the summer sky, and I had no degree. What I did have was a summer to remember. It was a summer of pure fun: working at the car wash, living the beachside party life, and chasing girls. Of course, none of those things would have been interesting without having been "one of the boys." Being one of the boys of summer trumped conforming to the rules of the classroom any day.

Summer has a funny way of distorting time when you're twenty-one, tricking you into thinking the carefree days and nights will last forever. As I rolled into work with my tunes up and my windows down, I caught a glimpse of a shiny new Mercedes parked at the market next to the car wash. While admiring this fine vehicle parked in the very spot my parents' van had seven years earlier, I watched a man exit it and walk towards the car wash office. I wondered who this man was. He was overdressed for work, and judging by the shine of his car, he was not in need of a car wash. What I didn't know was that he would soon be the owner of the car wash.

All of the boys at the car wash truly admired and looked up to Claudio and his partner Gaetano. They were going to be missed, and this made the change in ownership a difficult adjustment for everyone. In less than a month, the situation forced me to do something. I quickly readjusted the trajectory of my summer and my life: I quit the car wash and returned to school. I was saddened knowing that it was the end of an era. The car wash was no longer the place for me.

The following year, the sun seemed a little brighter as my graduate's cap sailed through the air and I clutched my degree. I was back to being my responsible self, and my parents were all smiles. It was a different story for my friends at the car wash, however. I had stayed in touch with them, and the picture they painted wasn't pretty. I had visions of them, a crew of lost souls aimlessly clinging to towels and wearily hoisting brushes with suds fizzling upon the bristles.

To my surprise, it wasn't long before the new owner and his general manager approached me about coming back to the car wash. I was intrigued. They explained to me that they were having a difficult time finding experienced and dependable people, and wanted me to give the business a jolt. Upon my return to working at the car wash part-time, my visions of the crew were closer to reality than I imagined.

A few months later, the general manager stepped aside. I wondered who would take his place until one day the owner invited me to his lovely new home on the edge of Lake Ontario. Of all people that I could have guessed, it turned out that it was I whom the owner had pegged for his top post. "Me? The general manager?!" I declined his offer. Twice. But he continued to up the ante, and I finally accepted his generous offer.

There I was, twenty-two years old and responsible for a $1 million+ facility employing twenty-seven workers aged from fourteen to sixty-nine. Both in title and in role, I was no longer one of the crew. What's worse, in their eyes, I was a sellout, a traitor, since now I was their boss. If I had any chance in engaging the employees and invigorating the business, I would have to learn how to quickly transition from being a foot soldier to a field marshal. A year of inconsistent leadership had left the business far from where the new owner imagined it would be. It was obvious that this team's dismal attitude was affecting the customer experiences. I therefore began to employ a famed U.S. military strategy: to win my people's hearts and minds.

Every workplace has a culture, even a car wash, and our culture needed a rebuild. I couldn't do this myself, and I knew it. My only option was to rally the troops and build a new one together. As is the temptation for anyone in their early twenties, I decided we would rebel. We weren't going to accept mediocrity, and we were going to give what the owner was looking for: quality and value. We would rally to continuously break revenue and volume records. We would fight it out together with a youthful spirit, developing a team akin to a band of brothers.

As our successes grew, the hearts and minds of the team were captured one by one. This approach motivated my slowly improving car-washing army. It also simultaneously altered the perception that their former coworker was not so bad after all. They viewed me more like a field marshal, a leader, and one who had their backs. And we won.

My team's sincere enthusiasm for connecting with people and active participation in all we did made our hard-earned success look easy. I learned that the basics of connecting with people had to come from within and that you *must* have passion and believe in your business and your people. If you don't have this, you are doing worse than just wasting your money. You are also squandering life's most precious commodity: time.

I remember my first one-dollar tip and how I learned to turn a service transaction into a service experience. My role as a young general manager of a car wash taught me that the real challenge was inspiring memorable customer experiences through leadership.

My second passion had been ignited.

Another New Shirt

After accomplishing my goals in the car wash industry, I was ready for a new challenge. I wanted to trade in my wet jeans and soggy boots for a clean shirt and tie. I decided to get into the financial services industry.

When you make a career change from one industry to another, there are a lot of uncertainties. Here I was striving to transition from being a kid from a car wash to becoming a financial services professional. I landed a position in a branch and began to work my way up. Two years into my new career, I applied for a new position that seemed like the perfect fit for me, and I ended up interviewing for it.

Remembering my mother's advice from my very first interview, I smiled, only this time without the shiny metal braces. How refreshing and comforting it was to see a bright and welcoming face beaming back at me. The woman interviewing me made me feel comfortable and had a smile that was contagious! Although she made me feel at ease, I couldn't help but notice a cloud of uncertainty drifting across the interview table. Something was off. She kept asking me the same question about my work experience at the car wash. I thought, "Did she not believe my answer? Am I not clear enough?" I just kept repeating myself to her. I presumed that she was attempting to shroud the same question under a veil of creative phrasing, as if I were being cross-examined before a court.

I truly was as passionate about my work experience at the car wash, as I was certain of its rich value. I believed that my decade in the car wash shaped me into the perfect fit for this new position. Unlike my "interview" with Claudio, this interview gave me plenty of time to explain why I was a valuable worker. I had an intuitive understanding that, regardless of industry, generational gaps, or social status, people were people, and people have choices. I learned that you must be empathetic and deliver the unexpected if you want to create memorable and delightful experiences. The more you focus on this, the more you are rewarded. Problems occur when leaders fail to set customer experiences as their priority.

I'm very thankful that, on my fourth and final interview, this woman who cross-examined me revealed that she was not one of those leaders. She exemplified her own fine attention to detail—and it drove me crazy. At the time, the interview seemed even more strenuous than ten hours of manual car wash labour. What was I thinking? She was persistent, and although I didn't quite appreciate it then, I now understand the value of her persistence. In her search for a sidekick, she would spare the frustration of no candidate. This job would be trying, and to ensure she had the right person, she would have to be a detail tyrant. I would eventually learn that this pursuit of perfection was not limited to her hiring practices. Her combing through the fine details in all she did proved to me that she valued customer experiences above all else. I liked this woman. Nothing would deter her. And when she gave me the job, I liked her even more!

When I reflect on the unexpected and memorable moments we've experienced since that day, and as I reflect on the time we spent building our customer service program, I can't help but think of the comment that Draj made to me during the Disney quality service workshop we both attended. As we posed for a picture, she leaned in and whispered, "We should write a book…."

I smiled for the picture and didn't immediately provide a reply, but I was thinking, "Sure, lady, and why don't we fly to the moon while we're at it…? Is she delusional?" But the deeper we got into our program, the more it became apparent to me. She was right. Our experiences were miles apart, and yet they always ran parallel. Regardless of the differences in job titles, industries, or decades dividing us, we learned the same lessons.

Since that day, Draj has taught me that you can move mountains when passion is partnered with positivity and enthusiasm. I believe we have proved that ever since she selected me as her co-pilot. Draj Fozard, the former bank executive, hired me, Jesse Otta, the kid from a car wash. From there, we began a journey weaving together stories old and new in a delightful, unexpected, and memorable fashion.

Chapter 3

Satisfaction Is
No Longer Enough

The Banker

Everyone wants satisfied customers, right? Wrong. It's no longer enough to simply satisfy your customers. Today, it's all about creating loyalty. Loyal customers, the ones who keep coming back and proactively refer family and friends, will do more for the financial well being and growth of your business than spending precious marketing dollars trying to attract new customers. According to Sergio Zyman in his book *The End of Advertising As We Know It*, "[i]t costs six times more to acquire a new customer than it does to retain an existing one." Moreover, "[a] 5 percent increase in retention rate can boost profits 25 to 125 percent." It is essential to focus on taking satisfied customers and turning them into loyal ones. The extra effort to create an emotional connection with existing customers pales in comparison to the costs of gaining new ones.

And the way business is conducted today has changed dramatically, even over the past few years, and it continues to evolve quickly. Main Street has become a global high-speed freeway. Barriers to competition have toppled with the entrenchment of the Internet, and consumer buying behaviours continue to change along with rapid technological developments in both hardware and software.

Businesses are now faced with delivering exceptional service through many different channels, both traditional and emerging. The term *omni-channel* is becoming commonplace as companies realize that customers will choose to do business in a variety of ways depending on their preferences and circumstances at any point in time. A customer might make a purchase online one day only to make a trip to the store in person the next. Omni-channel retailing refers to the integration of multifaceted customer experiences. This has led to companies moving well beyond traditional bricks-and-mortar. Online shopping, web/store integration, and apps for tablets and smart phones are becoming essential elements in doing business. Businesses are grappling with this technological convergence, as they recognize that a customer's impression of their service is actually the sum total of all touchpoints, perceptions, and experiences, regardless of how they connect.

Increasing consumer choices presses businesses to take on more responsibility and focus on ensuring the seamlessness, alignment, and consistency of the service experience. And if that isn't challenging enough, the savvy ones know they have to do all that while also finding ways to differentiate themselves from the competition. This is achieved through rewarding customer experiences. Products can be copied, but it takes people to make it personal and memorable. Being exceptional means being more than simply good: it's the wow factor, the unexpected, the kind of service that builds repeat business and lets customers know that the company appreciates their business.

Let's consider online shopping, for example. Consumers are basically anonymous online, and as such it's difficult to establish an emotional connection with them. They will quickly form first impressions about how user-friendly your website is, which may then influence their opinions about your company and/or your products. When problems arise, frustration sets in, and this may lead customers to form negative views that go beyond the website issues. In dealing with problems, instant chat and texting is becoming more commonplace, but their use is customer-driven—they either opt in or ignore it. If there is no option to interact directly, there is no opportunity for customers to ask questions, clarify information, or check for understanding. And if it becomes too much of a hassle, few online shoppers feel guilty when they abandon their shopping cart, mostly because of the lack of direct human interaction. It doesn't take people much thought to click away if they don't feel like updating their credit card information or if they're unsure about the specifications of a product. In other words, there is no one standing in front of them at a cash register. There are no physical products in a basket. There is no commitment like there is when a customer walks into a store.

When it comes to my own experiences as an online shopper, I must admit that I have very little patience when problems occur. When I have a problem, I want to easily find a help number, speak with a real person, and only have to tell my story once. Is that too much to ask? This is no different from the traditional customer who demands to be heard face to face. In these moments of truth, loyalty is either forged or destroyed.

Loyalty vs. Satisfaction

More and more companies are realizing that customer satisfaction is no longer enough and are turning to loyalty as a means of evaluating and measuring their customer service strategies.

A standardized measurement of loyalty widely used in many industries is the Net Promoter Score. In their book *The Ultimate Question 2.0: How Net Promoter Companies Thrive in a Customer-Driven World*, Fred Reichheld and Rob Markey demonstrate how the Net Promoter methodology drives loyalty and business results and how companies can also use it as an indicator of future growth. Some very prestigious and successful industry leaders have already adopted it, including Apple, Ritz-Carlton, Mercedes-Benz, and Avis.

In April 2013, I obtained my Net Promoter Associate Certification. The course was held in New York City. The attendees were from all over the world and represented a broad spectrum of organizations. I was intrigued to find myself sharing a table with classmates from a global insurance company headquartered in England, American software manufacturers, and even a vitamin producer from Rhode Island. They had all been charged with implementing and running a Net Promoter program in their workplace. I learned that our challenges were similar: Regardless of whether we did business through end-user or B2B relationships, building customer loyalty was more than just a matter of achieving a certain level of satisfaction. People and businesses have choices, and the competitive landscape is fierce.

Net Promoter is a simple measurement of loyalty and is based upon a single "likelihood to recommend" question. Customers are asked on a scale of 0 to 10 where they would be willing to recommend the product, service, or brand in question. The results are divided into three segments:

- *Detractors* are those who give scores between 0 and 6.
- *Passive* is for those with a score of 7 or 8.
- *Promoters* are those who give top scores of 9 or 10.

And here is the difference between a satisfied customer and a loyal customer. At a glance, a 7 or an 8 is a good score and a vote of confidence from your customer.

Customers who give such scores are obviously satisfied. However, there is a marked difference between these satisfied customers and your Promoters, the ones out there advocating for you. If something goes even slightly awry, the satisfied customers who are deemed Passive may not stick with you through thick and thin.

An effective customer loyalty measurement program involves following up with all surveyed customers to discuss their evaluation. Calling Promoters is easy. They are emotionally connected and love to tell their friends and family about you. Promoters are what all companies want; they help build businesses through their loyalty and advocacy. A simple phone call and thank you for their business goes a long way, as it builds goodwill and reinforces their role as Promoters. Calling Detractors, however, may not lead to pleasant or easy conversations, but for those willing to take chances, these calls can often be rewarding.

You can respond to the feedback of Passives and dig deeper into the relationship to find ways to improve on your service to them and ultimately wow them. It's possible to turn Passives into Promoters with the right strategy. Connecting with a Detractor can give you a second chance to fix minor issues or even deal with serious problems. Although this sort of thing isn't new in the realm of business, there is now a sense of urgency considering that social media channels facilitate the broadcasting of comments (both positive and negative) to thousands, and potentially millions, of people in mere seconds. Somehow, bad news always seems to travel a little more quickly. Consumers discuss their personal experiences emphatically, and this is especially so when it comes to bad experiences. Giving a customer a good experience is just meeting expectations. Smart companies are striving to deliver *exceptional* experiences, and this builds such a following that customers become almost cult-like. If you want to know what I mean, ask any Promoter of Disney or Apple what they think about their product and service experiences.

Loyalty? Cult following? I had no idea what all the talk was about until I started shopping for a new laptop.

Loyalty in Action

I met "Charlie" (not his real name) on my inaugural visit to the Apple Store in one of those suburban malls. Until then, the beehive of activity had always amazed me whenever I walked by the store. Bright lights, fine lines, and cool edges, it looked like a futuristic space station. Customers young and old marvelled at the newest designs, and the store glowed with a positive energy that didn't seem to come from all the lighting or even the screens on all the gleaming hardware. The day finally came. I was going to take the leap and find out what the hype was all about.

A satisfied Windows PC user for many years, I had always been hesitant about switching to an Apple. Perhaps it was my reluctance to change or a deep-seated insecurity that I was not "hip" enough, but on that day,

I stopped, looked in, and decided what the heck. I was going in to find out what my sons and friends have been raving about.

"Charlie," a twentysomething easily identifiable in his blue polo shirt, promptly and warmly greeted me with a huge smile. His sincerity was genuine; he looked directly into my eyes and made me feel like I was the most important customer in the store. Amidst all the buzz and activity that Saturday morning, I could feel my angst wash away. I knew it was going to be a good experience, but I couldn't have imagined that it would be as great as it was.

I readily admit that I'm not a technological diva; my brain is just not wired for creating Excel spreadsheets and the like. (I'm the one who gets to know the IT support team on a first-name basis at work.) However, I knew that I needed new equipment. I just didn't know if I wanted to spend over a thousand dollars on a new laptop, and I was concerned about navigating the learning curve of a new operating system.

It's no secret that Apple products aren't cheap, and opportunities to upsell to a not-so-savvy middle-aged woman are always in abundance. The forbidden fruit of deception was hanging from the tree, but "Charlie" didn't reach for it. It was rapport first, and business next. After taking the time to learn about me—my lifestyle, personally and professionally—he simply and clearly explained what my options were. Through his active listening and thoughtful questioning, he formed a complete picture of what my needs were—and, just as important, what they were not. There was no jargon or hard selling, and he tailored his style and vocabulary to mine. It was only after this was all completed that "Charlie" perfectly summarized our conversation and then provided his best advice and recommendation to me. Most important, his recommendation was in *my* best interests.

I was pleasantly surprised with my first experience at the Apple Store. I knew it was a sales interaction, and yet with "Charlie" it was more than that. It was different. There was no canned sales script or other mindless lines being repeated. You know the kind. The salesperson uses your first name in every sentence, and you wonder if they're using "fake genuineness" with you just to get the sale. (For the record, they are being creepy nonetheless.) Being immersed in the customer experience business, I find myself constantly and consciously analyzing customer service wherever I go. Whether it's a drive-through coffee shop or my favourite gas station, with every interaction and purchase, I'm making a judgement. I can't help myself. I know what's bad, what's good, and what's delightful. So after "Charlie" spent over an hour of his time with me, it came as no surprise to me that I felt a twinge of guilt when I told him I wanted some time to think about it. I was satisfied and thought I had the information I needed, but it wasn't enough for me to make the purchase.

The real test came next. To my delight, that wee bit of guilt was quickly erased when I noted the absence of overt pressure to make up my mind or attempts to close the deal that day. Instead, I received a business card upon which he took the time to write a personal message, which surprised me when I discovered it later. With another of his sincere warm smiles and hand-shake, "Charlie" thanked me for my time and for my consideration of Apple. I left the store with a new sense of confidence and excitement—confidence that I would be making a great decision if I bought the Apple laptop and excitement about all the features "Charlie" had shown me and the classes and tutorials I could sign up for. Expensive? Yes. But at that point, I wasn't even thinking about the price. That had become a non-issue.

It only took one visit to the Apple Store, and based on the personal and delightful service I had experienced, my decision was 98 percent made. The following Monday, as I relayed the story and raved about "Charlie" to my colleagues, it was reinforced again: Everyone loves Apple. I had no idea of the emotional connection that Apple advocates have for their devices. Until then, I had only heard or read about it. Now I too was becoming one of them, and I hadn't even made a purchase yet.

When I returned to the store the following week-end, "Charlie" remembered me, and I purchased the laptop. My experience to date has been nothing short of delightful in all aspects. Even when I had to call their service team with a question, they were marvellous. They translated the technical terms into words I could I understand, and they resolved my problem in that one call. I am beyond satisfied: I have become a loyal Apple customer. As a Promoter of all things Apple, I am truly in awe of the quality and simplicity of their products, and I won't hesitate to tell you.

People Drive Experience

Would I have purchased the laptop if my service experience had been a bad one? Chances are I would have defaulted to my zone of comfort and bought something familiar. I would have easily walked out of the store and perhaps gone with a new Windows laptop—a return to the road that was tried and true. I'm glad I didn't, and I'm glad it was "Charlie" who assisted me. However, something tells me any one of Apple's team would have been just as good. They attract, recruit, train, and motivate their employees to consistently deliver the kind of experience I had. It's not the latest tactic, or the "flavour of the month." Rather, their focus is on quality in all they create and do. It's their culture.

When face to face, the human element of interactions cannot be underestimated. Engaged employees quickly know how to connect and engage with customers on a personal level to find out what their needs are and to help them to find the right solution. The most memorable experiences happen when employees are empowered to go above and beyond the expected to find ways to delight. In doing so, they think of their work as more than "just a job."

Having witnessed this firsthand, I can confidently

say that my experience in the Apple Store was as exemplary as the quality of their products. The story of Apple's successes illustrates that customer satisfaction isn't enough. Many computer companies have satisfied customers, but Apple's customer loyalty rules the industry. Their success has grown on a strong and renowned foundation built by an incredibly mindful leader. The late Steve Jobs knew for a long time that Apple was more than just a computer company. Apple's ability to create a loyal and passionate following is what sets them apart from the competition.

Chapter Summary:
Satisfaction Is No Longer Enough

Loyalty vs. Satisfaction

- Measure loyalty, not satisfaction
- Talk to your customers and act on feedback
- Turn indifferent customers into advocates

Loyalty in Action

- Focus on creating a wow experience
- Make it easy for your customers to overlook the competition
- Sell solutions, recommendations, and advice, and the products/services will sell themselves

People Drive Experience

- Products can be reproduced, people can't
- Hire people who like people
- The work should be more than "just a job"

From mindless to mindful….

Are your customers loyal or simply satisfied?

Chapter 4

First Impressions Matter

The Banker

Our first impressions often lead to quick opinions about the people and things we come across. Admit it, you probably already formed an opinion about this book just by looking at the cover and reading the title. We hope it's an opinion that sparked your interest or curiosity.

There's no avoiding it. A first impression is powerful. Studies have shown that it takes us only seconds to form an opinion about the people we meet. These first impressions may be positive, neutral, or negative. Our reactions may be overt or subtle. Our minds process sensory information, and depending on the outcome, that first impression can affect everything that follows. This is one of the reasons why companies spend the time and energy to map their customers' experiences with a special focus on those initial critical moments—moments that matter.

For instance, when I began my career, banks didn't have a "welcome desk" or "help desk." That was unheard of. Everyone just lined up together and waited (and waited) regardless of the reasons for visiting. In today's banks, having a greeter or a reception area is now commonplace, and this is an essential part of the customer experience. Such service helps banks better understand their customers' needs beforehand so that customer traffic is directed efficiently and effectively. This in turn gives customers an impression of order and attentiveness— good things for a bank.

I first heard the saying "first impressions are lasting impressions" while working with one of my favourite branch managers and bosses of all time in the mid-eighties. He was such an excellent coach and mentor that I would have walked on burning embers or on shards of broken glass had he asked me to. That's how much I liked and trusted him. His words of wisdom guided me then and still remain with me today. His was the finishing school, the last stop before you had your own shop. He was well known for his legendary tutelage, and I was soon to find out what it meant to be one of his "graduates."

I had just been recently promoted to branch manager, and as I walked in to meet my new team on day one, my first impression was like a pail of cold water thrown at me. Sensory information indeed! No one was smiling, desks were cluttered with files and junk, and the only plant in the place sat dead in a corner. My excitement about my new assignment quickly disappeared, and I forced myself to keep smiling and stay in the moment. I couldn't let them see my true feelings. After all, my new team was also forming their first impression about me, so any handwringing or despair on my part wouldn't have been such a good idea. Thankfully, my positivity kicked in, and I was able to present a countenance of calm professionalism. Game on.

It turns out that there were some ongoing issues, but it wasn't anything that some focused attention and care couldn't take care of. While my first impression about the branch had been less than stellar, I knew I could turn the operation around so that future first impressions would be positive and engaging to all who passed through our doors.

That same week, I met Howard and his father. They owned a greeting card store complete with a post office located not too far from our branch in the mall. They had been our customers for several years and would come in daily to do their banking. In 1989, we shook hands for the first time, and I knew they were sizing me up. I'm sure they were thinking, "Another new manager…. Here we go again…." I, on the other hand, was forming my own opinion about them. My first impression was that they were really friendly, genuine, and very smart business owners. Howard's father, whom I guessed to be around seventy years old, had a twinkle in his eyes that made me smile. The service I experienced on my first visit to their store reflected their business savvy. This was a highly successful retail shop with a loyal clientele. It was such a friendly spot that I almost expected to see Norm from the television show *Cheers* sitting there during my subsequent visits. It was the kind of place where everyone knows your name.

We formed a solid business relationship, and it was a delight to be "their bank manager." In my career history, they rank among my favourite customers, so it was a sad farewell when I was transferred to another branch. As luck would have it, my new location was in the same city, so we stayed in touch. However, in 1994, I was promoted to a larger branch farther away, and as the years spun by, we lost touch with each other. That was until 2002.

In March 2002, I found myself with a new job at a new company in a new city. When I left TD Canada Trust, I had doubts that I would ever find a job in a financial institution with as strong and positive of a culture as the one I had left. I was wrong. I did find an organization whose culture matched and even surpassed what I had known. Welcome to Meridian Credit Union. I was a branch manager of a Niagara Falls location. I had been there a full week. I remember to this day sitting in my office late one afternoon when a great-looking couple walked by at the precise moment I lifted my head towards my open door. They were on their way somewhere, but I threw a smile and glance their way anyway. (Hey, I was the new manager.) There was something familiar about him, but nothing triggered my memory until I heard him say, "Draj? Is that you? What are you doing here?" I quickly looked up again, and although I had not seen him in almost eight years, I knew that voice and definitely recognized that smile.

It was Howard. What was he doing in Niagara Falls? I bet he wondered what I was doing in Niagara Falls too! We had a lot of catching up to do.

Howard had moved to Niagara Falls. Meeting Jolanta for the first time was a delight. Jolanta had been a member of the credit union for several years, but this was Howard's first visit, and it happened on my first week on the job. Coincidence? I don't think so.

They were there to apply for a mortgage on a unique house they had just made an offer on. Their offer was conditional upon financing, and the deal was time-sensitive. Long story short, I ended up securing the approval of the mortgage for them, and I was proud that Meridian was able to help make their dream come true. Twelve years later, the property is a warm and inviting home as well as one of the most popular bed and breakfasts in Niagara-on-the-Lake.

When Jesse and I were developing our customer service program and planning for this book, I felt that observing a B&B could give us inspiration and insight into the importance of first impressions. What are the challenges they face when striving to differentiate from the dozens of other B&Bs in the area? How do they go about creating a first impression that becomes a lasting impression?

At the corner of King and Centre Streets directly across from Memorial Park in the quaint little town of Niagara-on-the-Lake, you will find the Historic Lyons House Bed & Breakfast. It's a grande dame of a house, a stately and elegant structure surrounded by enchanting English gardens and century-old trees. Built in 1835 by John Lyons, a prominent lawyer and land registrar, it has been home to many families throughout the years. Today, Howard and Jolanta call it their home and share its history and magic with the many guests who come to stay there. For over twelve years, Howard and Jolanta, along with their two cats, Mr. Happy and Ruby, have welcomed guests from far and wide to stay for a while.

I was excited to introduce Howard and Jolanta to Jesse and to have an in-depth discussion with them about what they do to make it so special for their guests. The travel website TripAdvisor has consistently ranked the Historic Lyons House among the top 20 of 177 B&Bs. Proof of their tremendous success can be found in the many glowing reviews on the website, written by guests who have enjoyed the hospitality.

After work one day, Jesse and I paid them a visit. We had prepared a set of questions to ask, but between touring the house and grounds, meeting the cats, and having homemade cheesecake (complete with fresh raspberries), we never got to all the questions. But it didn't matter. The stories they shared with us about their experiences as innkeepers were so much more entertaining and insightful than anything we could have asked. We wanted to hear about what they do during those critical moments when first impressions are formed, for themselves and for their guests. What are Howard and Jolanta mindful of to earn such powerful and wonderful reviews?

Set the Stage

Howard and Jolanta first told us about their stage: their home.

The very first time they stepped into the house, they fell in love all over again, but this time it was the house that danced in their hearts. They told us that "it chose them" as much as they chose it. However, opening up a B&B had never been in their foreseeable future. As we all know, life is full of surprises, and not long after they moved in, Jolanta convinced Howard that opening a B&B would be a good idea. She knew that his natural curiosity about people would make him an exceptional innkeeper. He had also owned his own company and was well qualified to run a business.

That business today is focused on making their guests' B&B adventure both personable and memorable. They take great pride in their home and invest in quality and comfortable furnishings. So intent on creating a comfortable and interesting setting, they often move furniture around seeking ways to make the place a better experience. And judging by the original artwork and antiques, quality is a value they hold dear. There would be no dead plants at the Historical Lyons House!

After they warmly welcome their guests and introduce themselves, Howard and Jolanta quickly and mindfully ensure that new arrivals are comfortable and feeling good about their choice. They are particularly sensitive to those for whom it is their first time staying in a B&B. They know how important those first moments can be after a long trip. They tell guests that there is just one rule: Don't let the cats outside. The resident felines, Mr. Happy and Ruby, add personality and character. The ambience encourages guests to roam the house and its gardens and to fall in love with it just as Howard and Jolanta did.

First Impressions Go Both Ways

In the initial moments (and even before guests arrive), Howard and Jolanta expend much energy towards creating a positive first impression. However, as Howard recognizes and points out, "First impressions go both ways." As soon as the door opens, he and Jolanta are mindful that they too are forming their own impressions and opinions about their guests. They use this to help guide the conversation and respond to any questions. Howard has a degree in psychology, and Jolanta is a teacher. Both are experienced in reading people and situations. In addition to the detailed preparation for their guests, they use this small window of opportunity to their full advantage when people arrive. They take pride in their offering and strive to exceed expectations.

It comes as no surprise to see the Lyons House score perfect ratings in all six rating summary categories on TripAdvisor in addition to being awarded a "Certificate of Excellence" in 2014.

Little Things Mean a Lot

With so much competition in the vicinity, how is a stay at the Historic Lyons House B&B different from the rest? It's the little things. It's all about the details and the length to which Howard and Jolanta go to get things just right. The Lyons House is a portrait in detail. Remember the cheesecake I told you we had during our visit? It was served on exquisite bone china and garnished with a fresh sprig of mint. We weren't guests, but we certainly noticed and appreciated the extra effort. During our tour of the house, we noticed many beautiful flower arrangements. Small special added touches serve to make a guest feel special and appreciated.

Like Your Own Family

In a gracefully appointed dining room, guests enjoy breakfast together and sit at one table. It's a grand affair with great food, friendly banter, and laughter. New friendships are made, and some, we were told, continue to this day. Jolanta and Howard treat their guests like family. They recognize that everyone is different, and with subtlety and sincerity, they seek to discover what they need to do to make each stay special and memorable. This is a purposeful service strategy they use to differentiate themselves from other B&Bs in town. If someone wants to spend a day exploring the country roads visiting wineries, Howard readily offers suggestions, wine tasting coupons, and even the use of two bicycles—just what you would do for family.

Listening to Howard and Jolanta tell stories about their guests, it was obvious why they have been so successful. The care and concern they have for their guests, and the lengths to which they go to create a warm and welcoming first impression, is what sets them apart, and this is perhaps why half their guests return year after year. Their success is rooted in the work they put into making great first impressions. They know this is the first step in creating memorable customer experiences.

The Kid

My first memories of travel were of family vacations to new places that had the comforts and familiarity of home. Annual road trips to Florida included people who drove the same cars, wore the same clothes, and spoke the same language that I was used to. No matter what city we were in, home on the road was a hotel my father would carefully pick out for us. There was no TripAdvisor back then, so my father's instincts and first impressions guided his every decision. Once he picked a hotel, we would settle in for the night. They were all basically the same: cookie-cutter rooms, the scent of commercial cleaning products, and a deadbolt to keep strangers out, which made us feel safe. While I loved these trips with my family, and especially when I was pulled out of school, they didn't exactly turn me into travel enthusiast.

I wasn't bitten by the travel bug until I took a trip to Europe with my grandmother for the first time. After that momentous trip, I was off zigzagging across Europe with friends to explore different cultures, where the cars were strange, the clothes were nicer, and the languages were something other than my own. The one thing that remained the same during these trips, however, was that I was conditioned from a young age to stay in a North American style hotel with the deadbolt locked, making me feel safe and sound. No hostels or B&Bs for me. When it came to accommodations, I was a hotel guy. I always played it safe.

I was never interested in staying in a B&B, and I knew nothing at all about the business. When it came to B&Bs, all I had was an ill-formed idea that I would not be comfortable staying in one. My hotel room with the familiar layout suited me just fine. To me, what mattered was *outside* my accommodations. I would retire to the familiar comforts of my room when I was done exploring for the day. So when Draj wanted me to meet her long-time friends who owned one of the premier B&B locations in historic Niagara-on-the-Lake, it seemed like a perfect opportunity to gain some perspective. "What's the big deal with B&Bs?" the "hotel guy" in me thought. I was about to find out why B&Bs such as the Historic Lyons House attract so many guests from the far reaches of the globe and also how these establishments leave an impression on them.

It all started shortly after Howard opened the door to introduce himself. He studied me and related to me, but he really caught my attention when he told me that he too was a "hotel guy." We were getting somewhere. Beyond that, he was funny, which I liked, and he was quick to point out that he had a daughter named Jessi— a good name. We were only a few minutes in, and Howard already had three points on his "first impression scoreboard." Although he had already racked up those points, Jolanta entered the picture and scored the final points that would win me over. Sure, Howard did well enough, but Jolanta introduced herself with an offering of cheesecake. I liked Howard, but after Jolanta's sweet move, I think I liked her just a little bit more— the cheesecake was delicious!

Until I crossed their threshold, Howard and Jolanta were strangers to me. What I couldn't have understood during all those years staying in hotels was that strangers can sometimes be much less frightening than we imagine. Furthermore, those cookie-cutter rooms with the deadbolt that I was so fond of prevent you from getting to know new people, which is quite unlike the experience of a B&B. For many years, I was simply wrong in my thinking that culture was something that existed exclusively outside my hotel. Jolanta told me "culture is everywhere," and this is something I quickly learned. As we became acquainted, I realized that experiencing the culture of a country or a business had to start somewhere, and the first impression of that culture is absolutely critical.

Sitting in Howard and Jolanta's home felt like sitting in my own. Howard was a sharp and observant guy like my father, and Jolanta was obviously a future Michelin-starred chef like my mother. Most important, they were both good people. It felt as though they were my parents. That's the way they treat their guests—like their own family. Although the Lyons House was far removed from the car wash that was the setting of the formative years in my career, Howard and Jolanta's warm and welcoming first impression reminded me of my first day as manager of the car wash.

Upon returning to the car wash, I was looking forward to meeting the manager of the detailing shop. I had not yet met Dave, but his industry reputation in the area was legendary. I was excited to start my new part time job, as I knew I could learn a lot from a solid guy like Dave. As you may have guessed, the familiar feeling I had when I met Howard and Jolanta was a reminder of the day I met Dave.

Unlike the other side of the car wash, his shop was neat and tidy—he even power-washed the floor! His stage was his office, and his office was in order. Dave had a clean-cut appearance and looked directly at me when he talked to me. When I walked into the detailing bay to meet him, the first thing he did was introduce himself with a firm handshake. He then told me that he had heard good things about me. First impressions go both ways, I guess. He then gave me a tour of his shop and explained his philosophy on the car wash business. He even suggested how he could help too. This meant a lot to me. Before I headed home that day, as we were parting ways, the last thing Dave said to me was "I really look forward to working with you. You know, I have a son who is just about your age…." I felt like family.

My first impression of Dave made me even more excited to work with him. I liked him right away, and I liked him a lot. Like the warm and welcome feeling you get when you step inside Howard and Jolanta's B&B, stepping into Dave's shop feels like home. Auto detailing shops and B&Bs are worlds apart in two very different industries, but first impressions are formed everywhere. While Dave's detailing shop may not be an actual home like the Historic Lyons House, the way he makes you feel with his mindful approach to interacting with people, you wouldn't know any different.

Chapter Summary:
First Impressions Matter

Set the Stage
- Keep it clean and safe
- Make it warm and inviting
- Ensure it supports and is consistent with your brand

First Impressions Go Both Ways
- Listen for cues
- Do your homework
- Ask thoughtful questions
- Remember, you get what you give

Little Things Mean a Lot
- Details, details, details
- Go the extra mile but mind the inches
- Delight with the unexpected

Like Your Own Family
- Treat customers with empathy and care
- Make them comfortable
- Be genuine and sincere
- Find common ground

From mindless to mindful....

Is your personal first impression a lasting and positive one?

Chapter 5

Retail Is Detail

The Banker

It's amazing the amount of business jargon, acronyms, and catchy little phrases one can collect over the years. Leaders use them to create interest, direct focus, and send a message. I myself have found that the simpler they were, the better. The simple ones have lasting power. For me, there is one phrase that I find myself repeating over and over. Even to this day, if you walk by my desk, you will find "Retail Is Detail" written in bold letters on my white board. These three simple words have resonated with me and have had meaning for me (and hopefully those reporting to me) for many years. It has been my mantra. It's a constant reminder of a very important aspect of the customer experience in retail sales and service.

While I would love to take credit for its creation, I can't. It's a saying that's been around for years. My former boss and colleague at Canada Trust, Gary Ford, indoctrinated me with the idea that retail is detail. Before then, I knew what paying attention to detail was, but it was never a prominent blinking light on my management radar. Perhaps it had something to do with my perspective. I was much younger back then, and my lens was focused on seeing my world from the inside out rather than the outside in. The idea that retail is detail demands seeing it both ways. The widening of my management lens and a change in my perspective came soon enough. The opportunity for me to learn to see the forest *and* the trees came disguised as a promotion.

In my first assignment as a newly promoted branch manager, I began to understand the true meaning of these three simple words. Remember the first impression I had on my first day that left me almost speechless? The cluttered desks and that poor little dead plant made an impression all right—the wrong kind. When customers see things like that for the first time, they form opinions. Messy desks could indicate disorganized employees, which could lead customers to believe that they are careless, prone to errors, and possibly incompetent. Before you know it, a potential customer could become a missed opportunity if they decide their money isn't safe at such an institution. And this is all because of a few stacks of paper, misplaced files, and a dead plant.

First impressions form opinions and perceptions. Whether these are fair assessments or not, they can become a customer's reality—and yours. It doesn't matter if the employee with the messy desk is one of the friendliest and most capable in the branch, or the entire company for that matter. In the absence of a relationship, potential customers will default to their beliefs of what a bank should look and act like. The impression created in their minds is real to them. This aspect of customer service is too important to leave to chance.

Many years later, when I became a leader of a group of managers, I would often tell my reports that I thought they had the best job in the world. And I meant it too. They would also heard me say that leaders must be mindful about their responsibility and privilege to lead others and make a difference in their corner of the world. Great leadership requires managers who see from all angles and heights. Sometimes it requires getting into the weeds, and other times a manager needs to step back.

While focusing on details may appear to be a straightforward and relatively easy task to initiate, the truth is it isn't. Managers can create focus and lead by example through their own actions, but to keep things going requires a concerted and consistent effort from everyone. One person cannot do it all. For example, to ensure a standard of safety, order, and cleanliness, everyone has to pay attention to a multitude of factors. It takes a conscious effort to notice what may be awry or amiss. Especially when it comes to safety, all employees must look at the factors with a fresh set of eyes every day.

I learned from Gary that it takes significant energy

and effort to build a culture that values a focus on details. I have gone through the steps firsthand and would best describe the process as a driving force that captures the hearts and minds of everyone involved. Hiring the right people with a positive and willing attitude goes without saying, as having a highly functional team is essential to making it happen.

Establishing a focus on the details of your business will encourage employees to be mindful in creating memorable customer experiences. Maintaining this focus will set you apart from the competition; people will notice.

Details That Matter

Another common phrase that has proven its staying power is "moment of truth." Again, here are three simple but powerful words. These ones were popularized by a Swedish businessperson named Jan Carlzon, who wrote about his leadership experiences as CEO of Scandinavian Airlines in his book *Moments of Truth*. Published in 1987, the book's insights are still relevant. To this day, we recognize "moments of truth" as the opportunities to influence a customer's impression about a company, product, and/or service.

Today, organizations and consultants use the term and adapt it to their particular needs when mapping their customer experiences. The specific details of moments of truth between an airline and, say, an exclusively online company may differ, but the underlying commonality is that these are all moments that matter to the customer. An employee's or a manager's performance during these moments of truth will influence the outcome of customer experiences to range from "not a chance" to "okay" to "wow." During his stint as CEO of Scandinavian Airlines from the early eighties to the early nineties, Carlzon didn't have to deal with moments of truth arising in real time (and publicly) on social media. Customer communication is burgeoning on social media sites such as Twitter and Facebook. As companies grapple with this, they are finding that customer expectations are evolving. This has presented them with new and unique challenges in figuring out how to best respond.

Although communication technology has changed (and customer expectations along with it), reflecting back on my days in a branch still yields valuable lessons. There was one particular moment of truth that illustrates how big an impact little details can have on the total customer experience. Before the paperless transactional systems we have today, customers or tellers would have to complete deposit and withdrawal slips. For every transaction and for every account, you needed a corresponding withdrawal or deposit slip. Seriously. Most customers completed them. It was another step in the process for them. Contrary to popular belief, in the age of "in line" banking (before the advent of online banking), time was just as precious and scarce as it is now. As you can imagine, some found this process annoying, but they accepted it. They had no choice.

Customers would come in and fill out the slips with a pen that was usually attached to the counter. All the pens at the wickets and cheque desks were fastened with long dangly metal chains or heavy-gauge industrial-grade wire. (Yes, we had to protect ourselves from tricky pen thieves.) Now, aside from the obvious message this sent to customers—that we feared the pens being taken (accidentally or not)—there was another issue. Imagine the reaction when a customer walked in and the first pen they tried to use didn't work, but when they found another pen, it didn't work either. Both pens out of ink! This kind of thing could happen if someone forgot to change the refills. I have been on the receiving end of a customer's comments when this scenario happened. I totally understood how they were feeling. It would bug me too. A pen without ink may be a small detail for some, but it's more than that for others. Some who have found themselves in such a situation may have thought, "If they can't even keep their pens working, how careful are they with my money?" It's like the cluttered desks all over again.

Little details do matter. If you can't take care of the little things that matter, why would someone give you their business or trust anything you have to say?

In the quest for differentiating from the competition in service quality, companies must be mindful of everything that contributes to customer experiences. Years ago, it may have been a simple case of a pen being out of ink that created a negative impression in a customer's mind. Today, it could be a mobile app taking too long to launch or a company website being too difficult to navigate. The type of details may have changed, but our human perceptions and reactions are more than likely the same. Moreover, the sheer volume of messages and sensory information that we all have to process every day makes everything more challenging.

Everyone competes for people's attention and mind share. We are all bombarded by content. Our expectations are greater, and there is a certain urgency to life, whether real or imagined. Just think about how we typically greet one another. How often have you been involved in an exchange such as this?

"How are you?"

"Not bad. How are you?"

"I'm so busy."

Performing well during moments of truth that address people's busyness (real or imagined) will make a difference in their overall evaluation of the experience. Paying attention to the details can bring experiences from "not bad" to "wow."

You Get What You Settle For

One of my favourite stories about details comes from Disney, a company renowned for its relentless focus on details. In 1991, I had the good fortune to travel to East Asia. While taking the train in Hong Kong, I met a young woman who was on a business trip. She worked for Disney in Florida and was in Hong Kong to visit a supplier. The purpose of her trip was to personally verify a specific shade of the colour red. That was it. She had travelled over fourteen thousand kilometres on a twenty-eight-hour flight for the sole purpose of seeing if this particular red was a perfect match for Disney's specifications and expectations. Sitting across from her on the train, I thought about how important it must be to Disney to worry about such a small detail. They were willing to spend such resources of time and money to confirm a shade of red. Although I didn't quite understand the why of it all, I did recognize that there would have been other benefits of the trip. Establishing a personal connection with the factory supplying their goods would be a good thing, but it did seem a bit much to me at the time.

I remembered the young woman when I visited Disneyland with my two sons later that same year. My musings back on the train in Hong Kong were addressed during that visit to one of the most entertaining places on earth. Detail? There's nothing like Disneyland to demonstrate what attention to detail looks like. The bar at Disney is set so very high. They have become the gold standard, the example that so many companies study and aspire to. The standards of their customer experience model are admired and adopted by many. Walt Disney recognized that, "You can dream, create, design, and build the most wonderful place in the world…but it requires people to make the dream a reality." Continuing in the spirit of Walt, his people showed me just that in 1991, and to this day, they still recognize and value his words.

I have yet to attend any customer-related workshop where Disneyland and all things Disney didn't come up in some way. Even in my own workshops and seminars, someone always mentions Disney when the group is asked about personal examples of memorable customer experiences. Whether you're young or old, it's a rare occurrence to leave the theme park without having felt something magical during your visit. Memories are made at Disneyland, and that is one of the reasons they are held in such high regard.

The Disney team doesn't settle. They didn't have to send an employee halfway around the world to check out a colour sample, but they did. They have decided that even small details are important to their business model. They know that they must do everything a certain way to create magic for their guests. This means getting the details exactly right—all the details.

Talk Less, Listen More

Humans are brilliant. The average person talks at a rate of about 125–175 words per minute, while we can listen at a rate of up to 450 words per minute.[1] What is amazing is that we can do it at the same time. However, according to the International Listening Association (www.listen.org), we tend to derive far more meaning through non-verbal cues and tone of voice than we do through the words themselves. You may be wondering how this affects the process of creating mindful customer experiences. It's simple.

Just because you hear what someone is saying, it doesn't mean you're listening. You can hear someone talk but be thinking about or doing something else. You can try to pay attention, but your inner dialogue might interrupt your train of thought even if it's triggered by what the other person is saying. Your mind then wanders as you think about your own experiences as they relate to what you hear. You're not in the moment. When engaging with customers, you have to do more than just hear them out. You must also recognize all the non-verbal cues and other messages being sent. This means talking less so that you can listen and observe more.

Effective listening means removing the filters we all possess. It means listening without interpretations and judgements. For instance, external factors such as the age, appearance, and voice of the person you are interacting with can influence how you listen. How you listen to your spouse, your boss, and your child differs. Sometimes your focus is more on the messenger than the actual message.

Active and effective listening is achieved when you are fully present. To deliver memorable experiences and have genuine personal interactions with others, you must "show up." Your demeanour should demonstrate your interest, you should use appropriate body language, and your mind should be fully engaged in the moment. This is easier said than done. As the saying goes, we're given one mouth and two ears. We need to talk less and listen more.

I have learned how to listen well thanks to Gary always keeping me on my toes. This means I engage with people by purposefully listening with an open mind and avoiding contributing to the conversation with personal opinions or stories about myself. A common conversational habit is a kind of "echoing," like when someone listens to you only to promptly respond with a similar story that they experienced. When this happens to you, perhaps you wonder if the person even heard what you said. A better conversational practice is to stay quiet except to ask questions. Let the focus and attention remain on the person who's currently speaking. In doing this, I notice and hear details I may otherwise miss. I try to avoid thinking about what to say while waiting to speak. I remain in the moment and demonstrate respect and genuine interest in the other person. This practice will make you a fantastic listener, and people will appreciate it because engaging with such a listener is memorable, as I have learned.

More than ten years ago, I attended an offsite training course called the Leadership Path. It was a week-long session that taught leaders new skills to become better leaders. In my group was "Matthew" (not his real name), a company lawyer for a prominent customer loyalty program. Although this was a while ago now, I remember that week like it was yesterday. "Matthew" was a gentle soul. He was tall and extremely intelligent, and I noticed his very expensive Cartier watch. He asked me the proper pronunciation of my name. He was so interested in my name. The little details. Needless to say, we hit it off.

It's amazing how the dynamics of an interaction can change when two people find common ground. "Matthew" and I clicked, but what made him memorable was how he made me feel. His ability to focus on me while I spoke to him was remarkable. He had such sincere intent, a steady gaze, and positive body language. I couldn't help but conclude that he must think me the most interesting person on the planet!

"Matthew" demonstrated the power of listening and created an opportunity to discover details about me that perhaps I wouldn't have shared otherwise. Although we had just met, we shared such a natural and comfortable conversation. I have never forgotten the many conversations we had that week, especially considering the way he quietly listened to me. I liked this lawyer!

Keep It Simple

There are thousands of books written about customer experience—how to develop it, implement it, and improve it. Just google "customer service," and you will get tens of millions of hits. In the past few years, there has been such a proliferation of blogs, sites, and articles all devoted to the topic.

There are many training programs and consultants available. Information overload is evident, and budgets are limited. There is knowledge to be gained, but there is no guarantee that insights will lead to the successful implementation of a customer experience strategy. What's a company to do? The answer is obvious: Keep it simple. The buzzwords may have changed decade to decade, but the basic tenets of creating a delightful and memorable customer service experience have not.

One of my favourite quotes is one attributed to the late poet Maya Angelou: "I've learned that people will forget what you said, people will forget what you did, but people will never forget how you made them feel." The words are simple, but the message is profound. People have feelings, which means customers have feelings. With every interaction with every customer, regardless of whether it's face to face or through technology, an impression is made, and it's the little details that count. These impressions will be positive, neutral, or negative, and they are influenced by the emotional responses customers inevitably have to their experiences. As much as we'd like to think we're rational beings, we cannot completely separate our emotions from our thought processes. This is important to remember because the customer experience is the sum total of all of the little things.

Yet, no matter how simple this is as a concept, the practice itself is not. The rules are changing. With recent advances in communication technology (both in hardware and software), we now communicate differently and with less formality. Our attention spans have shortened, and our impatience is on the rise. In our beleaguered, text-driven LOL/emoticon world, some may say the art of conversation is on a downward spiral. We're quickly moving to what I like to call a heads-down society. On subway trains, in restaurants, and even out in green spaces, you will usually find someone with their head down concentrating on their smart device, oblivious to the world around them.

Thankfully, all is not lost. This brave new world requires a renewed energy and focus on ensuring that time-honoured traditions and true values of courtesy and respect remain and, furthermore, remain relevant. Manners do matter. The simple use of *please* and *thank you* shouldn't get lost even in the shuffle of abbreviated and rushed communication. They should be non-negotiable in a face-to-face chat, a telephone call, an email, and even in text messages.

Calling customers by name is another simple activity that will make a difference, as will keeping your promises. So if you tell someone you will call back on Wednesday at 10 a.m., then *call back*. This was important to customers thirty years ago, and it's just as important today. Although the means by which you contact people have changed over the years, people's expectations haven't.

Gary taught me to never miss an opportunity to thank and/or recognize customers and staff. A prince of a guy himself, he certainly knows how to make everyone feel special. An Annual Award of Excellence Celebration was held each year in our region at Canada Trust, and Gary was in charge, overseeing every single detail. I remember my first year as a presenter. I was nervous enough as it was, but to make matters worse, Gary called me into his office beforehand. "Uh-oh," I thought. "Now what?" He had me rehearse my speeches in front of him. I practiced repeatedly until he was satisfied (and I was exhausted).

The awards evening turned out to be a fabulous success. Everyone played their part, and I read my lines perfectly. But what was particularly memorable was what happened during the closing remarks. Gary made a point of sincerely thanking and recognizing every single person—by name—for the part they played. It was very powerful. He took the time, he knew the details, and he expressed his gratitude sincerely. I have carried this lesson with me ever since.

Never miss an opportunity to say thank you.

Thank you, Gary.

The Kid

Managing and working at a full service car wash was no walk in the park. In fact, it was rigorous work—physically grueling and mentally exhausting. After ten long years at the car wash, I had accomplished all I had set out to do and more. I was ready for a change and excited at the prospect of a new challenge. I thought the car wash may have pushed me to the limit, but realistically I didn't know what I didn't know. How could I have known my limit? I hadn't been pushed far enough. That all changed once I met Draj.

Draj pushes me every day and in all sorts of ways. There is no "mailing it in" with her; you always have to be on your toes and bring your best self to work each morning. I couldn't get away with handing in any work without her asking, "Is this the best that you can do?" And when things didn't go as planned, she would gently ask, "What did you learn? What are you going to do differently next time?" With her encouragement, I discovered just how capable I was. I learned that I could go further than I could have ever imagined.

While she was busy teaching and pushing me, Draj was also hammering different messages into my mind. One in particular stands out above all others. It's her guiding principle, her succinct mantra: "Retail Is Detail." I couldn't escape from these three words if I tried, as I would hear them quite often, even if I plugged my ears. I couldn't avoid seeing them in large print on her oversized whiteboard:

RETAIL IS DETAIL

No one could miss these three words plastered across her whiteboard, and if you didn't "get it" the first hundred times, she wouldn't hesitate to tell you.

I was indoctrinated with Draj's beloved mantra on

my first day, but it didn't stop there. As I continued on in my new job, I would visit many branches and attend various meetings, but no matter where I went, those three words would often surface. I have heard branch managers, regional directors, and other senior leaders repeat Draj's three favourite words a surprising number of times. When they did, they would usually credit Draj as the source of the mantra whether she was present or not. Her championing of "retail is detail" had obviously touched many others throughout her career. Everyone seemed to apply it to just about any situation good or bad. When things went exceptionally well, it was the detail that made the difference. When things didn't go so well, it was usually because someone had tripped over a small detail. We refer to those as the "pebbles." Little things make a difference—both ways. Retail is detail: I couldn't escape those three words! It was the cult of detail, and Draj was the leader of it all. Or so I thought….

I have always believed in the power of mentorship and that for great things to be accomplished mentors always play a critical role. This belief rang true the day I met Gary Ford. Draj wanted to introduce me to her former boss and colleague, so we decided to meet for breakfast at a café near the edge of Lake Ontario on a sunny Friday morning. I could see that even this wise former banker to whom I was now reporting didn't get to where she was without a mentor. Gary's influence was instantly recognizable, and even though it had been years since Draj reported to Gary, he was still pushing her. We talked about our customer service philosophies, and he challenged Draj to think differently about certain aspects of her own. When you speak with Gary, he may do a lot of talking, but there is no shortage of listening on his part when it truly counts, and he doesn't settle for less than perfection.

The scene unfolding in front of me was very familiar but had an added twist. I've been in the hot seat many times, but now Draj was in it. I observed my mentor in the place of the mentee for a brief moment, and I was quite entertained! Gary wasn't letting her off easy. He's skilled at asking tough but thought-provoking questions, and they were well intended. In the end, she held her own.

Draj had passed Gary's tests, but it became very clear that the mantra "retail is detail" was a product of Gary's teaching over the years. However, it was what he said next that made me almost leap out of my seat in excitement. He pointed at my iPhone that was resting on the table and said, "If you want perfection, you've got it sitting right there on the table. Talk about an organization that is focused on the details!" As a long-time fan of the extraordinary attention to detail that Apple puts into all facets of its products and retail experience, I knew that Gary was right on the money. I really liked this guy.

We sat there on the patio of the café, with a cool breeze from the lake at my back. Peering over Draj's shoulder, I couldn't help but notice Gary's shiny new

Audi in the parking lot. It made me think of the car wash. I thought about my past life and how it fit into the context of "retail is detail." In the car wash industry, it is fair to say "retail is...detailing"! I could completely relate to what Draj and Gary both were saying about the details. When it came to the car wash, detail was our *entire* business.

As Draj and Gary were catching up with each other, my mind continued to drift back to the car wash. Before I had Draj's famed mantra drilled into my mind, I had a boss who was to me what Gary was to Draj. My boss was Jeff Morabito, and he was instrumental in helping me develop a sense of mindfulness when it came to the little things. Jeff was a guy you couldn't help but like. He was one of a kind, incredibly creative, and always finding new ways to make everyone laugh.

Our maintenance pro was a guy named "Derrick" (not his real name). He would come by the car wash to fix some ailing equipment and would always call himself "the Doctor." A doctor? Of a car wash? It was as funny to us as it was absurd, but we all joked that the Doctor was in the house whenever "Derrick" came by. In good fun, Jeff would imitate "Derrick" by letting me know that he too was a car wash doctor, only instead of machinery, he would operate on quality.

Jeff was always perfecting the small details. He constantly mentored me and, without me even knowing it, taught me lessons through his humour. Whenever I missed anything, it was Jeff's keen eye for quality that caught it, and he would bring it to my attention using humour. He would even ask me if I too wanted to be a car wash doctor just like him.

Jeff would always tell me that it was the little things that mattered, and he made everything relevant to me as a sixteen-year-old by keeping my attention and keeping me laughing. I admired how Jeff could remember every regular customer's name along with specific car wash preferences. Newer customers would always be pleasantly surprised by this, and Jeff's attentiveness always gave them a reason to come back. If "Dr. Jeff" was working, customers were assured that they would get exactly what they wanted, right down to the last detail. As we know, retail in the car wash business is "detailing."

Being mindful often requires inspiration from peers and/or leaders, and this is especially true when it comes to the little things. I was so fortunate to have someone like Jeff around to provide that inspiration to me by leading by example.

Thanks to Gary, Draj, and "Dr. Jeff" for being leaders that zeroed in on the details. Through them I continue to be inspired and creative.

Chapter Summary:
Retail Is Detail

Details That Matter

- Be ready to seize the "wow" moment
- Walk a mile in your customer's shoes
- Adjust your lens
- See the forest *and* the trees

You Get What You Settle For

- Have a relentless focus on getting it right
- Value quality
- Don't settle for anything but your best
- Ask yourself "Would Disney approve?"

Talk Less, Listen More

- Listen and understand
- Ask questions to confirm
- Maintain eye contact
- Don't interrupt

Keep It Simple

- Manners still matter
- Use names and be courteous
- Be engaging with a friendly and pleasant tone
- Never miss an opportunity to say thank you

From mindless to mindful….

Do you see what your customer sees?

Chapter 6

Culture Is Everything

The Banker

Shortly after Jesse and I attended the quality service workshop held by the folks at Disney, we began creating and planning our customer service program for work. We thought we could run a pilot in a few branches to test it out. We were fairly confident about what we wanted to do, but we wanted to conduct as much research as possible to make sure we covered all the important aspects.

As we discussed the organizations we admired in addition to Disney, it was easily decided that we would not have to travel to Florida (as much as we would have liked to) but instead to nearby Niagara-on-the-Lake! What we were looking for was actually right in our own backyard. The White Oaks Resort & Spa is an established and highly regarded destination in the Niagara region. Throughout my banking career, I had many a meeting and workshop there. I had even been involved in organizing several galas and conferences there. Having had many experiences at White Oaks, I recognized that they would be an ideal organization to focus on as a glorious standard to aspire to.

I have always marvelled at their relentless attention to detail and, more important, their consistency in performing well at that level. It seemed to be in their cultural DNA. Much to my delight, it turned out that Jesse actually knew Ameer Wakil, the owner of White Oaks, as a long-time customer of the car wash. Whether it was a coincidence or not, Ameer's son eventually worked at the car wash and became a good friend of Jesse's. Surely this was meant to be a sign of good things to come. Ameer graciously accepted our invitation to speak with us. So it was with that in mind that we carefully prepared our questions for him. We were set to discover the secrets of White Oaks' success and learn about their culture. We would soon hear about a culture so well understood and so embraced by their employees that it has become the heart of the organization. I was excited about finally meeting the man behind the magic.

My excitement was partly influenced by having heard him speak several years ago. It was at a Christmas luncheon, and he was the keynote speaker. He engaged the audience with such a memorable story that it became one I use myself whenever I need to illustrate what delivering a "wow" customer experience looks like. When the folks from Disney asked for an example of such an experience during their packed workshop, I gladly repeated the story to a room full of strangers. It's a true story about how, on a hot summer day, a car with

American license plates pulled up to the front entrance of White Oaks. Inside was a couple looking weary and a bit frantic. The man asked the doorman if his wife could use the facilities, as she was not feeling well and needed a rest room right away. The man readily admitted that he and his wife weren't guests but were on their way home to the United States. The doorman quickly responded with a "yes, of course" and personally escorted the poor woman to the facilities while her husband waited at the car in the visitors' parking lot. So far so good. We would all like to be treated with that same level of kindness should any of us find ourselves in the same predicament. However, what makes this story so special and memorable to me is what happened next.

When the woman came out, the doorman greeted her with a smile and a small bag containing two cold bottles of water, one for her and one for her husband. This little added touch is what makes White Oaks so special. This was the doorman's "moment of truth." The bottles of water not only represent going beyond the expected, they also serve as symbols of the culture at White Oaks, which is a culture of employee engagement and empowerment.

But it didn't end there. The man whose wife was treated with such kindness and who enjoyed that complimentary bottle of water turned out to be a CEO of a corporation in the United States. Guess where he arranged to hold the next annual company meeting the following year? White Oaks. That small act of kindness by the doorman was not forgotten, and it resulted in a good business opportunity.

Why is this so important?

Competition in the hospitality industry is fierce, especially in the Niagara region. With hundreds of hotels and B&Bs competing for the same tourist dollars, they all look for ways to differentiate themselves. They focus on building loyalty and growing their businesses through word-of-mouth referrals and advocacy. One only has to look at the reviews on such sites as TripAdvisor to realize how powerful words can be. Reviews can have a tremendous impact on the business and future bookings. The positive ones will certainly help sell rooms, but the negative commentary can be outright disastrous for the business. That's the power of the Internet and social media today. It's an undeniable force that requires new ways of thinking and responding.

We've all heard the saying "walk a mile in my shoes." Building a mindful customer experience requires doing just that. This means shifting your perspective and looking both ways: from the outside in and the inside out. Effective leaders put themselves in both their customers' and their employees' shoes. Change your perspective, and you will see differently. And it's important to think beyond what you see; be sure to also purposefully think about what you *don't* see.

Strong leaders shift their perspectives as required. This means getting into the trenches if necessary, but it can also mean quickly climbing to higher ground. It's about knowing the appropriate time to adjust your view of the business from the close details to the big picture. When you do this with purpose and a thoughtful intent to learn, the insights you gain will be all the more valuable.

Our interview with Ameer revealed that he is a mindful leader and that he and his 550+ employees have an unwavering dedication and determination to finding ways to delight their guests. As illustrated in the story about the doorman, anyone who visits White Oaks for any reason will be treated in first-class fashion. Whether it's for a one-hour meeting, a drop-in lunch, or a week-long conference, every guest is special. This doesn't happen by chance, or when employees happen to be in a good mood. It's a deliberate strategy that the White Oaks team has operationalized with passion and conviction.

From the doorman who greets you upon entry to Ameer himself, the folks at White Oaks all strive to shift their perspectives, anticipate needs, and to "walk a mile in their customers' shoes." They recognize that they are in the business of making delightful memories for their guests. This focus works. Our interview with Ameer during our visit at White Oaks is another delightful memory, and learning some of the secrets of their success only made it that much better.

Empowerment

White Oaks' success is partly the result of empowerment programs such as I Make It Right (IMIR). Every employee can use their judgement and discretion to spend up to a pre-established amount to correct a wrong or treat guests to an unexpected delight. There's no need to explain or ask for approval from a supervisor. They are empowered to execute one-stop resolutions and are encouraged to exercise their creativity. Ameer shared an example of a cleaner from housekeeping who overheard two guests in an elevator commenting about the noise from another room and being disturbed by someone loudly pounding on the door in the early hours of the morning. The employee politely asked if they could provide her with any details. When they did, she said how sorry she was for what had happened. Later that same night, a bottle of wine and a fruit basket was delivered to their room along with a handwritten note of apology wishing them a better evening.

Ameer believes that in his world "there are no mistakes, just lessons." He shared that story with us as he did with others. All IMIR stories are summarized each month and discussed by senior management in an effort to learn and improve. In the case of the two guests who were disturbed at night, management investigated further and learned of a late-night party that was held on the same floor. They asked themselves what they could have done differently and what they needed to change in the future to avoid a repeat occurrence. Their solution was to adjust their current procedures, to react sooner and implement an early warning system. They discuss the IMIR stories to determine the underlying themes for repeat issues and make adjustments along the way, all in an effort to simply do it better next time.

The IMIR program also serves as a means to recognize their employees, who are actively engaged in seeking out opportunities to make things right. Each employee's capacity to act when a moment of truth arises brings the wow factor to those who pass through White Oaks' doors, and management acknowledges that any positive feedback from guests comes as a result of individual employee actions.

Ownership

In addition to employee empowerment, Ameer believes that the other ingredient fundamental to their success is ownership—at all levels and in all positions. Employees are empowered to make decisions and are held accountable for their outcomes. It's a simple formula that White Oaks has operationalized successfully. For instance, the human resources team handles recruitment, but managers have direct accountability for hiring their own teams. This ensures managers are involved and are responsible for their own decisions and people.

At White Oaks, the tenure of over half the employees is over five years. That's an impressive statistic, especially considering the high turnover rates in the hospitality industry. Ameer attributes this to the way his employees are treated. He beamed with pride when he told us about a recent retiree who had been with the company since 1978. She had retired to spend more time with her grandchildren, and in her thirty-four years, she had never missed a day of work with the exception of an emergency. He admired her discipline, but, most important, he appreciated her and told us he considered her "to be a blessing." These days, thirty-four consecutive years of service is a rare feat. So how does White Oaks go about recognizing their employees today?

Recognition

At White Oaks, it doesn't stop with empowerment and ownership. Recognition has a starring role in their unique culture that has been built over the years. Ameer described their employee recognition program called the White Oaks Winners in Excellence (WOWIE). Teammates throughout the organization can reward each other whenever they witness outstanding and exemplary service, be it to each other or to guests. These simple yet powerful acts recognize and celebrate each other, further strengthening relationships, promoting teamwork, and reinforcing the message about keeping the magic alive, for themselves and for their guests. Being appreciated is a fundamental human need, and recognizing employees for performing good work validates the role they play and indicates their value. This in turn increases their job satisfaction and motivates them to do more and do it better.

At White Oaks, recognition and praise are essential to building their outstanding work environment. The White Oaks leadership walks the talk. They know that being respected and valued for effective contributions is essential to their team's engagement. They know that making people feel good about themselves and their work improves employee retention. Empowerment, ownership, and recognition—all of these are important pillars of the culture at White Oaks.

As Ameer finished the WOWIE story, I watched our server. She was looking after Ameer, Jesse, and me and had brought us a bottle of San Pellegrino mineral water and a small plate of thinly sliced lemons and limes. She poured the water into each of the three glasses and then placed the bottle on the sleek granite coffee table. That may seem simple enough, but what she did next had me smile in recognition of her attention to detail. After she put the bottle down, she turned it ever so slightly so that the label faced us properly. She eyed it to make sure it was perfect. She then noticed the flower arrangement and delicately arranged the gerbera daisy in the vase.

Ameer greeted her by name, and they struck up a friendly conversation. The personal connection was not difficult to spot. She smiled at us all with the same sincerity. Guest or CEO, it was all the same. She certainly knew who he was, but, more important, he knew who she was. Right after she left, Ameer said, "This is the simplest thing ever, but very few people get it: A happy team member is a happy customer. It's so basic. I can't do everything. I can't clean the rooms. I can't be everywhere. But what I can do is make sure my team is happy.

If an employee is miserable because of their manager, then how in the world will they treat the guests?" What a wise man he is.

White Oaks is successful because of its people and the culture they have built. The leadership team strives to ensure that all employees understand it, embrace it, and are willing to protect it. How employees work with each other is just as important as what they do. Their supportive culture allows them to make decisions and not second-guess themselves. Feeling valued and important, they don't have to think about whether they should or shouldn't take action, and they know they will be supported either way. Someone always has their back.

This is a culture that provides employees with absolute clarity on the values and service standards that White Oaks holds dear. All that is required is mindful execution. This formula for success works because everyone knows their role and is purposeful in the overall delivery of the guest experience.

When we asked Ameer to comment about the White Oaks culture, he said, "The fish rots from the head.... If the leader is lousy, the culture will follow suit." That made me chuckle. Wow, did he just say that? I sat across from him in a plush velvet chair while strains of a Frank Sinatra song floated in the background. I watched him as he spoke. He was impeccably dressed. His gaze was direct, and his words were emphatic. I doubted very much that there were any fish rotting in this resort. This leader makes the promise of the White Oaks brand come alive. Ameer is the heart of the culture, and he believes each of his employees is an integral part of the fabric woven into that culture.

Why did I feel so special sipping on my Italian mineral water? When Ameer spoke to me, I felt like I was the most important person in the room. He reminded me of "Matthew," the lawyer I discussed in the previous chapter. Ameer even managed to notice and comment on the Tiffany bracelets I wore. His focus and attention to detail in our brief meeting was quite extraordinary, and I wondered what drives him to reach this level of perfection. When I asked him, he simply said that he feels totally responsible for the livelihood of all his employees and their families. He considers them his White Oaks family. This is what motivates him to get up in the morning and go to work every day. It's his way of contributing to the world.

Did Anyone Wow You?

The White Oaks team actively engages in evaluating their performance. One way they do this is through a disciplined mystery-shopping program that provides valuable feedback. This program isn't seen as an overhead expense but rather an investment in continuous improvement. It provides an objective opinion on all aspects of the operation and guest experience.

The evaluation questionnaire that the mystery guests complete is a valuable tool for the management team. The questionnaire is quite comprehensive and measures both logistical considerations as well as the experiential and emotional aspects of the stay. The results are summarized, discussed, investigated, and eventually acted upon. As Ameer says, "There are no mistakes, just lessons."

The last question on that questionnaire is "Did anyone wow you?"

From my perspective, yes, Ameer, you most certainly did.

The Kid

As Draj and I pored over examples of great customer experiences while developing our customer service program, one organization that kept coming up for both of us was White Oaks Resort & Spa. White Oaks was the standard-bearer in our minds. We have both tried to model White Oaks to some degree at the car wash and at the bank in our vastly different careers. Draj eventually asked herself a question out loud: "Wouldn't it be fabulous if we could sit down and talk with the owner?" I thought about it, and she was right; it sure would be nice.

While searching for someone else to meet, I eventually told her that we should talk to a guy I knew from the car wash who happened to know a thing or two about building a culture. I didn't tell her who it was. All I said to her was, "If you want an expert on building a culture, I know a guy…." She was in. I set up a time for us to meet and kept the person's name a secret from

Draj until a few days before our meeting.

So who was this guy, anyway? Well, before I tell you, there is a bit of a background story to explain.

If you drive about sixty kilometres southeast of White Oaks, you'll find yourself in Buffalo, New York. Buffalo is uniquely identifiable by its interesting culture, including its cold winters contrasting its warm and friendly residents. It's the birthplace of the spicy Buffalo wing, it's rich in architectural history, and it's the home of the NHL's Buffalo Sabres. I've made the short trek many times to watch Sabres games and experience the best of Buffalo's culture. Thanks to these trips, I had also made an important connection. I'm grateful that many of the trips were with my former co-worker and long-time friend Jamil, but we also travelled with one of our favourite car wash regulars. That guy I told Draj I knew? He was that car wash regular, and he happened to be Jamil's father, Ameer Wakil (or Mr. Wakil, as I refer to him). Yes, the owner of White Oaks!

During these drives, we would talk about the things we were passionate about: our love for the city of Buffalo and our boys in blue and gold, our families, and, of course, our work. Sitting in the car en route to the arena and back, I would learn much from Ameer, and I could seek his advice on any matter concerning the car wash. He was a car enthusiast himself who kept his personal vehicle spotless (I admire that) and had an unmistakable passion for all things service related. Best of all, he loved to provide guidance when needed. How fortunate was I to have the person who built one of the most well respected organizations in the Niagara region as my unofficial (and unpaid) "chief advisor"? It was priceless… quite literally.

White Oaks may be vastly different from the entire city of Buffalo, but like Buffalo, it too has its own interesting and identifiable culture. The employees of White Oaks view their work through their spotless cultural lens. It gives them the perspective they need to view things the White Oaks way. However, if you were to find any marks on this lens, it would be Ameer's fingerprints. From the neat and tidy appearance of 550+ employees to their spotless fleet of vehicles, the staff and Ameer are one and the same, woven together to create the fabric of White Oaks. Their culture also extends far beyond the superficial. It's not just about the neat and tidy cars and perfectly pressed shirts. It's about the way the people working hard under the White Oaks brand make you feel; it's the way they care for and respect their guests.

Pablo Picasso said, "Good artists copy, great artists steal," and I knew that if I were able to steal even a few ideas from Ameer, our car wash culture could be a great one. However, stealing a few ideas turned into an all-out raid of the White Oaks' cultural treasure chest, as I wanted to steal from every aspect I could. I wanted to achieve greatness for the car wash, so to kick things off I started with our look.

If we were to be taken seriously as a car wash of exceptional quality, we would have to look the part. We couldn't be the stereotypical rag-tag crew with dirty shirts and depressingly saggy pants. Would you want someone who looks like they can't wash their own clothes to clean your car? Could there be anything worse? Surprisingly, the answer is yes. There *can* be something worse. Being worse means taking that same rag-tag group and forcing them to wear a tacky uniform. *Voila!* Now you have a miserable-looking group of mostly teens and twentysomethings hoping their standard-issue car wash uniform bow tie ends up choking whatever life is left in them. They will be too depressed and distracted by how silly they look to want to face a customer. Imagine a staff member mindlessly uttering, "Welcome to the car wash…" while thinking only of being invisible to customers while wearing something so embarrassing. Goodbye engagement.

The car wash staff would have to feel good about what they were wearing, like the folks at White Oaks do. I would have to meet everyone halfway. So what did the owner and I do? We bought designer polo shirts in bulk and added our logo. These shirts were smart-looking, professional, and yet cool enough that you would be more than okay with being seen in one—you'd actually *want* to wear one. Since the shirt was cool even with its logo, it felt less like uniform propaganda and more like a badge of honour. The confidence this badge of honour gave to each staff member helped them show customers their pride in being a special part of the car wash.

Like White Oaks, we couldn't get by on just the superficial. We looked and felt good, but we needed to do more than that to truly build a culture. The crew needed to feel empowered, and to get there I had to help them realize that their contributions made a difference. This realization would foster an environment where their empowerment would infuse everything they did—most important was their interactions with customers. So we started a beautification project of the car wash facility itself, and my crew was now in charge. They were the new gardening architects. It was up to them to decide on what flowers to hang or plant to brighten up our environment. They were also responsible for the maintenance of the grounds. The crew was empowered to figure it all out. They built confidence and a positive feeling as they saw their hard work bloom (no pun intended). Their newfound sense of empowerment that they derived from shaping the environment around them translated into more confident customer interactions. They now felt a part of something that they had created.

So how did Ameer teach me about the importance of recognition at the car wash? It was during my first year in university, and quite frankly it wasn't even through Ameer directly! I learned through Samir, who was my best friend since childhood. He was a newly hired employee at White Oaks. I knew Ameer and some of the White Oaks team through our interactions at the car wash, so it was no surprise to me that Samir continuously raved about working there. I almost immediately saw the White Oaks culture begin to rub off on him.

Samir had been very new to the organization, not

knowing very many people outside of his team of porters in the conference centre. One day, a man impeccably dressed in a suit asked Samir if he could briefly join him in his office. The man introduced himself as Ameer Wakil, the owner of White Oaks, and he started a conversation to get to know his new employee. He asked Samir about his educational goals, about his career aspirations, and, of course, how his early experience had been at White Oaks. He recognized Samir as an individual, and he thanked Samir for his work as an important member of the White Oaks family even though he was still relatively new. He finally let him know that his door was always open if he needed to talk. He treated Samir like a VIP guest at the resort. How is that for hospitality?

With 550+ employees, it's difficult to recognize each person individually, but this is something Ameer strives to do. The personal attention and recognition that Ameer gives his team is leadership by example. Ameer treats his staff with the same level of attention that his guests receive, and this raises the bar for everyone to reach. As someone on the outside, I have always aspired to reach Ameer's example as a standard for leadership.

Recognition of my car wash crew for their individual efforts was one of the most powerful tools that I had as a leader. You can't imagine how gruelling a ten-hour car wash shift in the dead of a Canadian winter can be to even the toughest people. Recognizing each employee always seemed to add an extra spring to their step to help them through the tough days. I knew that if I could put a smile on the faces of my crew and make them feel appreciated, it would be passed on to our customers and they would feel the same. An appreciation of the staff means better customer service and a better chance to succeed like the White Oaks team does every day.

This is why each and every year Ameer, Jamil, and I cheer and praise at the top of our lungs for our Buffalo Sabres. We hope that they too remain a winning organization!

Chapter Summary:
Culture Is Everything

Empowerment

- Lead by example
- Trust your employees
- Provide front line support the power to say yes more often

Ownership

- Fix what's broken—make it right
- Correct your course as necessary
- Pair seasoned employees with new recruits

Recognition

- Celebrate the big and the small
- Timing is everything—catch people doing something right
- Make it a big deal
- Appreciated staff means appreciated customers

From mindless to mindful....

What do you want to be known for?

Chapter 7

Words Become Worlds

The Kid

I may have had a bit of a swagger in high school due to my affiliation as one of the boys of the car wash. While I remained an honour roll student who was respectful of my elders, such swagger inspired me to look at things differently. I became a challenging contrarian, sometimes to the ire of my teachers. This was especially evident during my campaign to run for student council president, where I learned the true power of words. In the end, I won the election by a landslide, but what was truly extraordinary was that I accomplished this using a grand total of only nine words during the speeches. Yes, nine words—no more, no less.

My opponent was a bright young man who loved history and politics. His grandfather was a Canadian war hero, and there was no doubt that his passion for history and patriotism was embedded in his DNA. He had been on the student council each year since he entered high school, and he racked up a long list of academic achievements. He was a very articulate speaker who excelled in debates. From an academic standpoint, he was presidential material and was thought to be a shoo-in for the election. I knew I had my work cut out for me, since by comparison I was that kid who worked at the car wash who quit the student council in the ninth grade. (Hey, more time for me to wash cars and make money.) The deck was stacked against me.

Know Your Audience

The day before the election, my fellow students filed into the auditorium as all of the candidates from each grade sat nervously upon the stage. Each candidate had the opportunity to speak. We were to tell the students why they should cast their votes for us. We were to inform them what we would do for the school if we won. Grade by grade and position by position, the speakers pleaded their cases until it was down to the final two: me vs. the ideal candidate.

As the final two, we would duel for the one single seat as student council president, and I was up first. In the days leading up to this moment, I stressed over what I could possibly say. My high school academic achievements weren't at the same level as my opponent's, but I was also worried because he was a master in the art of the debate, and I had to live up to my track record of having bailed on the student council in the past.

But then it hit me. My opponent, the distinguished Mr. Academia, dominated the bulletins as a model student who won award after award. The student body was sick of hearing about him and hearing from him. I needed to be fresh, and to do that I had to become an antihero, with my car wash swagger and all. So I stepped up to the microphone with my entire speech memorized, and I let the school have it—all six words of it: "Vote for me because...*I rule!*"

The school erupted with cheers and laughter, and I felt the rush of energy from my brief but successful performance. Although it was a great reaction, I still figured the battle was not yet over. I knew my counterpart would be prepared with a fiery speech that may rival the reaction that I got if the student body wasn't completely sick of him. What I didn't expect was that his speech *would* have been a fiery speech if he were delivering it to an auditorium filled with teachers. Unfortunately for him, he didn't appreciate that his audience was an auditorium filled with high school students.

The crowd sat in silence as my opponent rambled on for a good five minutes about what he planned to do as president. He then came to a point in his speech that *should* have spelled doom for me. He turned his head to his left to look me in the eye as he asked the school, "Why would you vote for the person who quit the student council in the past?"

This is the moment where everything changed. My speech was all of six words, but my next three would seal our fates. I seized the moment, leaped out of my chair, and proclaimed, "*Student council sucks!*"

The school roared to life! Their antihero was born,

and it was game over for Mr. Academia. I learned two things in that moment: 1) know your audience, and 2) even a few words (in this case, exactly nine) can become worlds.

The first words spoken to me after I sat back down were from my long-time friend and fellow student council candidate Miranda Voth, who said, "Congratulations! You just won the election." Miranda happened to be right on the money, as I won the election the next day. As the years went on, Miranda and I remained friends, and whenever she's given me advice, her words have continued to be right on the money.

Words, as it turns out, have become Miranda's world and her life's work. After high school, she went on to Ryerson University to study journalism. Upon completion of her degree, she ended up working for a few creative marketing agencies. Today, she works as a social content strategist for a Toronto marketing agency, and she lives a lifestyle as a fashionista and urban socialite blogger (www.mirandavoth.com).

Along the way to her current position, Miranda has shared many stories where words have become worlds, be it negatively or positively. One of these stories always prompts me to think of the late Heath Ledger's portrayal of the Joker, Batman's nemesis, in the 2012 film *The Dark Knight Rises* when he asks a criminal rival, "Why so *serious*?"

Miranda's story taught me exactly why words and their timing are, in fact, "so serious." Words said too early, too late, or just simply in the wrong context can turn a simple question or comment with innocent intentions into an insensitive and emotionally charged utterance. In Miranda's story, she didn't have the same luck with timing as I did with my ad lib during my opponent's speech for student council president. However, exactly like my own speech, Miranda's story revolves around precisely six words.

Miranda had been working on a campaign around the time of the release of the 2012 blockbuster film *The Dark Knight Rises*. This included managing her client's Twitter account. True to her form, she was hard at work bright and early…even on a Friday! The date was Friday, July 20th, to be exact. In an attempt to get her client noticed through the buzz and social media conversation surrounding this epic film, Miranda tweeted out six words that would teach her a great lesson about the power of words: timing is everything. Those six words were formed as a very simple and innocent question: "Has anyone seen the Batman movie?" What's so wrong with that Tweet on its own? It's just a basic yes-or-no question about this popular new movie, right?

Wrong—*very* wrong. To know exactly why, you would have to rewind the calendar a bit further to the previous evening, mere hours before Miranda's ill-fated tweet. On that night, Miranda was out on a date in the city and hadn't paid attention to current events. (For good reason, of course!) While she was enjoying the evening with her date in Toronto, a heavily armed twenty-five-year-old Ph.D. student entered the Century movie theatre in Aurora, Colorado, and took the lives of twelve innocent moviegoers attending the Batman movie. The heartbreaking murders included people aged from six to fifty-one, and seventy others were injured in the brutal attack. *Very* serious indeed.

The backlash for the tweet was immediate, and one could only imagine how horrible Miranda felt. She had relevant content, but unbeknownst to her, it was delivered at the most inappropriate time. She issued an immediate apology and explanation, likely shortly before I received the text from her that read, "You WON'T believe what just happened...."

This example highlights how crucial it is to be mindful of what's going on directly around you *and* around the world. In his famous TED Talk *Pop an ollie and innovate!* multimillionaire entrepreneur Rodney Mullen, the godfather of street skateboarding, says, "Context shapes content." In the wrong context, your content—or, simply, the words you choose—may not be received as you intend it to be. What on the surface looks like a positive message can turn out negatively. Context matters.

As important as it is to know what's going on locally and globally, it's also important to be mindful of your immediate surroundings. Just imagine a mother with a young daughter in tow about to pay for a car wash only to overhear a lewd or otherwise inappropriate remark from a car wash attendant. What kind of experience is that? That's more than enough for such a customer to storm out of the car wash and never return. Even if there were a time and place for that kind of remark, it certainly would never be in the workplace during hours of operation. Keeping aware of the workplace environment and acting accordingly ensures no such embarrassing (and potentially damaging) situations arise.

Don't Eat Your Words

Having grown up in Canada, I can attest to the tremendous influence of American culture on Canada through media and business. Much of our media selection is dominated by American companies, which naturally feature a significant amount of American advertising. One such advertisement for a new product available for a limited time had Canadian fans of Taco Bell in quite a tizzy. The new Doritos Locos Tacos was available in America, but Canadian taco aficionados were left empty-handed. It was nationalistic Taco Bell fan discrimination! Canadian Taco Bell fans took to the Internet to vent their frustrations. They sent angry tweets and Facebook messages to the official pages of Taco Bell in Canada. Not only did they demand to know why the Doritos Locos Tacos wasn't available north of the border, they demanded the product be made available to them.

Luckily for Taco Bell, it was the very same brilliant agency that Miranda works for who had the answer for Taco Bell *and* their angry (and starving) Canadian fans. As it turns out, the Doritos Locos Tacos had already been planned for roll out to Canadian Taco Bell restaurants a few months after the U.S. launch of the product. It was a perfect time to capitalize on the attention and backlash of Taco Bell customers and make them eat their own words…quite literally.

The agency collected all the angry feedback and invited each outraged Canadian to a special event that Taco Bell hoped they would be able to attend. The agency also used a special laser machine capable of burning the angry quotes onto Doritos Locos Tacos shells. The quotes were carefully burned onto each shell before being prepared for consumption. The attendees of the event were served tacos bearing their very own complaints, and the Angry Doritos Locos Tacos was born. They were served exactly what they wanted, but they were forced to eat their own words in the process.[2]

What a completely surprising and memorable experience these fans got. Miranda's agency turned angry fans into stunned advocates. They took a public debacle and built it into a brilliant campaign. The campaign's overwhelming success made the limited-time offer so popular that it became a regular menu item. Taco lovers rejoice!

Now, I can't say that I would advocate ramming customers' complaints down their throats and making a joke out of it. The point here is about being mindful of the power that your words have to be engaging, surprising, and even inspiring enough to create a lasting memory.

Of equal importance is listening and being just as mindful of the words your customers use. Take, for example, the woman who owned the convenience store between my home and the car wash. She was always a fun customer, bringing her sense of humour each time she visited the car wash, and going into her store was always a treat.

One particular morning felt a little earlier than usual due to an evening of fun I had with the boys from the car wash. I needed a little something extra to put a jump in my step, so I decided to stop at the convenience store to buy a can of Red Bull. As I paid for the drink, the woman who owned the store made an off-the-cuff remark about how it would be nice if someone could pick up her car while she was working and wash it for her. We both laughed before it struck me. It *would* be nice. So I asked for her keys, and told her I would take care of it. Surprised, she told me that I didn't have to do that for her and that she was only kidding. But the bottom line was that she wasn't kidding. It's exactly what she would have wanted, but she felt it was impolite to ask. I told her that she was right, that I didn't *have* to do it, but it would be nice, and being nice was a part of our reputation.

Her words meant something, and while I didn't

write them in soap on her car, and what I did wasn't a grand gesture, I believe I gave her a convenient experience that she would tell her own customers about and hopefully would not soon forget.

The Internet Never Forgets

While people sometimes forget things, my social content strategist friend Miranda is always quick to remind me that one thing is for certain: The Internet never forgets. Whatever you or your organization posts online will be archived indefinitely, so you better listen to the wise old proverb to measure twice and cut once. Beyond any posts that you control, your customers and the general public have the power to take your offline words and put them online. It makes sense to be mindful of the fact that just about everyone has a small camera capable of both stills and video at the ready in their pockets. Smart phones come with such camera capabilities by default, and if smart phones aren't ubiquitous yet, they're certainly on their way to becoming so. You never know when the spotlight is on you or your people. In today's world, the words you choose to say to one person can easily (and practically instantly) be made available to billions of others through the power of the Internet.

There have been many examples where a YouTube video or a tweet has gone viral much to the chagrin and embarrassment of the individuals and organizations involved. In some instances, it has cost people their jobs and destroyed their reputations. Public relations firms have had their work cut out for themselves and their clients, as the rules of the digital world are still in their formative stages. Responding to such online embarrassment has become the new frontier for public relations firms. The world was a very different place the day I made the outrageous statement that "student council sucks." If I had made that same statement today and one of my peers were to post my proclamation (out of context) to YouTube, it would likely come back to haunt me. Fortunately, I know a brilliant social content strategist should such an occurrence arise!

The Banker

When I met Miranda, it was her lipstick that I noticed first. A beautiful shade of deep red, deftly applied, it was the perfect frame for the generous smile she offered me as she shook my hand and proceeded to sit across from me at the table. Jesse had arranged for us to have lunch at the Queen Mother Cafe, a most hip bistro on Queen Street West in Toronto. It was a popular spot teeming with young professionals. Black was the popular colour to wear, and everyone engaged in deep conversation with their entourage...or their mobile device. Ah, the big city.

Jesse and I were interested in learning more about the ins and outs of managing customer service in the social media universe and were delighted that Miranda had accepted our invitation. It was interesting to hear her talk about her work, her blog, and the experiences she's had creating and managing the social media aspect of different brands.

I especially appreciated the opportunity to view the world from her perspective and to get some insight into where it was all going. Twitter, Instagram, and Snapchat have become prominent channels for voicing satisfaction, but more often than not they are used to share displeasure with a company, product, or service. Jesse was already quite familiar with such platforms, but being that I was more comfortable with the more traditional channels of communication, I wanted and needed to learn about Miranda's world.

Miranda and Jesse had attended school together in St. Catharines. Even though she eventually moved to Toronto, they had kept in touch like most kids do these days thanks to Facebook and the like. Everyone is now but one text, one post, or one email away.

The company and conversation turned out to be delightful and quite informative. Miranda impressed me with her smarts, candour, and confidence. Above all, she impressed me with her focus! Unlike the people seated at the tables around us, no one at our table checked their iPhone or BlackBerry during lunch. So when we planned our customer service program and book, it was obvious that it would be a good idea to get to know Miranda a little more and to tap into her knowledge. As Jesse has already illustrated, she knows up close and personal the power of words, that words can be mindless or mindful.

In addition to the power of timing and the power knowing your audience, here is another insight I would like to share that has served me well throughout my career and even at home. I first learned about this at a workshop presented by my good friend Gary Ford. He also writes about it in his book *Life Is Sales*.

This insight is concerning the phrase "no problem," especially when used as response to "thank you." To illustrate this with a real-life example, I'm reminded of some of my past credit interactions with customers. Applying for a loan or mortgage can be an uncomfortable experience for some, especially if they have what we politely refer to in the business as a "colourful" credit history. In these situations, I remember working especially hard to put together a deal and get it approved. If I believed in my customers, I would do everything in my power to help them out. I would step up to the plate and go to bat for them. In the cases where I hit a home run and got the approval, I always looked forward to making the call to my customers to let them know they were going to get their dream home or drive that car they'd always wanted. Their credit application was approved! This was a wonderful part of my job. The customers would then thank me profusely, to which I believe I replied, "You're very welcome." I still say that today along with some other powerful words I have learned along the way

However, the world is changing, and it's becoming apparent that as communication technology becomes less formal, our language is following suit. The shift to casual language has affected communication norms, and personal conversations are a reflection of this. It seems our abbreviated staccato LOL/OMG world is here to stay. This personal usage is also quickly bleeding into business usage. One rather casual modern-day phrase of both worlds is "no problem." Gary points out that there is now a tendency to say "no problem" to everything. Everything is no problem? Really?

Being in the service business, I can't help but critique all my personal service experiences. I decided to purposefully listen for this phrase. Gary is right. It has become ubiquitous, and I've noticed another phrase is on the rise as well. I don't know where it came from, but it's similar to "no problem." I increasingly hear "no worries," usually from the younger generation. For example, I went out for dinner one night and happened to ask for ketchup for my fries. After receiving the bottle of ketchup, I politely said thank you to the waiter. The response? "No worries." No worries?

Why say that? Did I look worried? Truth be told, I *am* worried about a few things in life. As a mother, I worry about my two sons. As an animal lover, I worry about what trouble my two cats might get themselves into. As a citizen of this planet, I worry about global warming and the depletion of our resources. These are things worth worrying about. When it comes to ketchup, however, worrying is the furthest thing from my mind. "No worries" as a response, while innocent and probably well meaning, annoyed me—the customer. It was probably said without thinking, a moment of mindlessness perhaps.

I will admit that "no problem" and "no worries" might have a place, and such responses might be appropriate in some instances. However, the issue is what impact such words have on the receiver. Why is this important? Like the title of this chapter, words become worlds. What would have happened had I said "no problem" instead of "you're very welcome" to my customers? What impression would I have made on them? Certainly, by saying "no problem," I wouldn't have done myself any favours. To reply with "no problem" after receiving a heartfelt thank you from a customer who has just heard life-changing news might actually give the impression that I put relatively little effort into the situation. To say something like that is to miss an opportunity to build emotional equity.

My coaching for service professionals includes finding ways to leverage important moments. One way is to easily replace "no problem" with two other simple but oh so powerful words: "My pleasure."

"No problem" vs. "my pleasure." It's a world of difference.

Chapter Summary:
Words Become Worlds

Know Your Audience

- Do your homework and personalize your approach
- Calibrate your tone and language
- Remember, it's about them, not you

Timing Is Everything

- Stay on top of current events locally and globally
- Measure twice and cut once
- Apologize swiftly and sincerely

Eat Your Words

- Welcome feedback and view it objectively
- Look for the silver lining in the storm cloud
- Statements are made for a reason—understand what customers are truly asking for
- Say "my pleasure" instead of "no problem"

The Internet Never Forgets

- Once it's out there, it's out there forever
- Global is the new local
- Cameras are everywhere—choose your words wisely

From mindless to mindful….

When is the last time you ate your words?

Chapter 8

The Personal Connection

The Kid

When we ask children what they want to be when they grow up, in many cases, the answers seem absurd. A Disney Princess? A Ninja Turtle? Beyoncé? Before I became a kid working at a car wash, I was used to hearing people laugh at me whenever I answered this question. My answer? A professional wrestler. No one ever took my answer seriously, probably because I was a skinny kid. My childhood hero was Hulk Hogan, but I was nearly two hundred pounds shy of a build such as his, and so my prospects of becoming a pro wrestler seemed bleak.

Being that I was used to the mockery of those who heard my grandiose future plans, it came as a shock when someone took me seriously. It was my grade eight teacher Mr. Strickland. He saw things differently. He didn't laugh at me. Instead, he looked me in the eye and wanted to learn more. Years later, I would discover that Mr. Strickland didn't care much for pro wrestling. So why would someone who paid no attention to this often bizarre form of live theatre care to learn more about it? It was because it mattered to me, his student. It was a childhood dream, and having one is something Mr. Strickland was well acquainted with.

Mr. Strickland's classroom was over 6,600 kilometres away from his own childhood dream. His classroom was very different from what he envisioned as the setting of his life's work: the Oceanographic Museum of Monaco. An architectural gem that protrudes from a picturesque rocky cliff, the museum overlooks azure blue waters that crash along its base. Monaco itself is amongst the most glamorous and desirable (not to mention expensive) two square kilometres on the planet. If that isn't enough to make this museum special, the legacy of its past director certainly is. The late Jacques Cousteau was and still remains the most well known oceanographer in the world. From the age of five, young Colin Strickland aspired to one day become an oceanographer just like his hero.

Mr. Strickland had just about everything it took to do it too. He was bright, curious, and motivated, and I'm willing to bet that he even had a few powder-blue shirts and red toques tucked away in his closet. He was on his way to worldwide oceanographic fame until he made his very first underwater discovery: He was afraid of the deep end of the pool! Nine feet of chlorinated terror forced Mr. Strickland to abandon chasing schools of fish in the sea, and he instead ended up chasing kids in a school—a school that needed him much more.

Since Mr. Strickland would not be submerged in the oceans researching and discovering, he would do the next best thing: teach. To teach effectively, teachers need to have the full trust and attention of their students. Building trust requires establishing strong personal connections. For Mr. Strickland, achieving this meant using a collection of skills that he developed and refined over the years.

Today, I am very thankful for the year I spent in Mr. Strickland's grade eight classroom. I didn't realize it then, but he had taught me so much more than history, math, and Canadian geography. The following year, I would start my career in the car wash. There I would begin to develop some of the same skills my teacher had demonstrated to his students every day. As I reflect back, I now know these skills all contribute to making personal connections. Mr. Strickland had taught me the importance of sharing your story, focusing on a positive perspective, and knowing the magic of staying connected.

Share Your Story

Working in a convenience business like a car wash is much different from teaching in a classroom. Even with such a stark contrast, some of the things I learned from Mr. Strickland were evident years later in the way I developed relationships with customers and employees.

As essential as it was for Mr. Strickland to get to

know his students, it was important to him that his students knew who he was as well. By allowing us to get to know him as a person, he showed us a level of respect we weren't used to. Most teachers I had up to that point led very private lives outside of the classroom. Without knowing much about their interests, hobbies, or social life, it was difficult for me to imagine them as a person outside of an educational environment. All I knew was that Ms. or Mr. Teacher was at the school before I arrived, taught lessons all day, and stayed until after I had gone home. Mr. Strickland was different. We knew Mr. Strickland as a person. We knew he was interested in basketball, design, and skateboarding. He wasn't afraid to share his story, and he proved to be real and credible. We trusted him. Mr. Strickland was cool, and we liked him.

Our feelings about him weren't accidental. They were a result of Mr. Strickland's approach. His approach was the same then as it is now. He lets his students see him as not only a teacher but also as a person. The more that students get to know him, the better chance they have at connecting in a meaningful way. Once students connect, it's only natural that their level of engagement increases as they become receptive and trusting. By being honest and genuine about himself, Mr. Strickland's credibility allows him to captivate the attention of the classroom.

So what could this possibly have to do with a car wash? How would I take what I learned in the classroom and apply it to the business?

Sharing our story began a year into my run as manager of the car wash, shortly after a major disaster struck. This disaster wasn't in the car wash tunnel. In fact, it was nowhere near the car wash. It was about 2,800 km away from it. In January 2010, a 7.0-magnitude earthquake struck near Port-au-Prince, the capital city of Haiti. This was a disaster of epic proportions that destroyed approximately 250,000 homes and took hundreds of thousands of lives. This event was significant to the car wash because one of our most dedicated employees, Reynald (known as "Joe"), lost his uncle when his family's home collapsed. Joe's entire family of sixteen were now homeless. Joe, who was helping to support his family, felt helpless being so far away. He was frantic and worried beyond compare. And so were we. How could we help him? What could we do? That day, I called an impromptu meeting, and we all met right after work. It was clear that we all really liked Joe, and though he didn't have family in Canada, he had us—his car wash family. We would be there to help.

I asked the team if they would be willing to donate the day's tips towards some costs that Joe was sure to incur, such as long-distance phone calls. What happened next made me so proud that to this day I still get goosebumps whenever I think of it. The team agreed to donate their tips *for the whole week*. And as if that wasn't enough, they also donated some of their hourly wages. This series of selfless acts showed me that this team had extraordinary character. At the time, I thought it would be an absolute shame if this story remained within the walls of the car wash. I felt compelled to share it.

I called up Don Fraser, who was a car wash customer and a friend. He was a business reporter of our local newspaper, and I told him what the team had done to help Joe. I felt that our story should be shared so that the team would receive the recognition they deserved. Arrangements were made, and soon a crew from the newspaper arrived to capture the moment. We surprised Joe that day and presented him with a cheque for $2,000. Tears of both sorrow and joy flowed. The next day, the story was front-page news. It was even picked up by other papers and car wash trade association news outlets. This was a first in nearly twenty years for the car wash.

For the first time, the community to which we belonged knew who we were and how big our hearts were. My intention for sharing this story was simply to recognize my team and the character they showed. Being in the paper was a nod to a hardworking group that did the right thing. To the surprise of Joe and the kindhearted car wash staff, they would receive much more than recognition than that. As an unintended result of our story being published, the community wanted to be a part of the story too. Suddenly, the cars flowed to the car wash en masse. Readers of the paper wanted to come in to meet Joe and the team. And the community didn't forget about Joe's kindhearted co-workers who gave up their tips and pay. The tips flowed generously, nearly quadrupling the average tips for many days following.

I learned a valuable lesson that week. Relationships become stronger when personal stories are shared. Relationships with customers are a two-way street, like any other successful relationship. It doesn't matter if you're teaching a group of grade eight students, working at a car wash, or managing a store in a mall; nobody will fully trust a person or entity they don't know or aren't familiar with. Conversely, customers will gravitate towards those they feel they understand. Being mindful of sharing your story will help you become real and credible in the critical early stages of creating a personal connection.

A Positive Perspective

I was only twenty-two years old when I became the manager of the car wash. While my team ranged in age from fourteen to sixty-nine, the majority of the staff was in their teens and early twenties. In most cases, this made it easier for me to connect with my car wash crew. However, there was one staff member named "Richard" (not his real name) who was sometimes a challenge for me.

Like Joe, "Richard" was a hardworking and dependable employee. He was effortlessly cool, which made him popular among his co-workers. By the age of twenty, he already had four years of car-washing experience under his belt. When he was on his best behaviour, he was a great example to the other staff, and you could see he had leadership potential. When things didn't go his way, however, his potential was disguised and his attitude became a distraction to the whole team. "Richard" had a short fuse, and his temper would turn him into a loose cannon. In a way, I could relate to him. While I may not have been a loose cannon, in my younger days, I admit I was impatient and sometimes acted out immaturely to express my frustration.

So how did others deal with me when I expressed my own frustration? It all comes back to Mr. Strickland. When he knew that a student's attitude was going sideways, he would coach them to view things with a positive perspective. He was always practicing this in the classroom and working to plant the seeds of positivity in his students. It wasn't uncommon to see pictures around the classroom of highlights and achievements throughout the year. Those pictures were strategically placed to boost the confidence of the students, but they also reminded them of the possibilities of their achievements. If a student was having a rough December, all Mr. Strickland would do is point to a picture from November's achievements and let them know that he believes they can be as great as they were in the picture.

Whenever my patience wore thin and I was frustrated in Mr. Strickland's classroom, instead of throwing a fit, I would become the class clown. Whether it was appropriate or not, I thought that making people laugh was better than putting my fist into a wall. Yet, Mr. Strickland knew that if he came down hard on me, it would only increase my frustration and he would lose me. Doing that would make him just another teacher telling me what I was doing wrong. Instead, he would challenge me to see the bigger picture. He would remind me of my past achievements and ask me to reflect on them. Then he would give me time and space to adjust my behaviour and let that positive perspective sink in. More often than not, improved behaviour was exactly the result he would get.

Remembering Mr. Strickland's approach, I began to apply what I had learned to "Richard's" situation. I would praise "Richard" on all his achievements, knowing I would need to remind him of them one day. And sure enough, that day arrived when "Richard" became frustrated at having fewer hours on the schedule than he had expected. As a way of expressing this frustration, he decided to drop his pants, revealing a full moon in plain view of a customer! The customer was a sweet elderly woman who may have been about the same age as "Richard's" own grandmother, who had raised him. She let out a giggle that turned into an all-out laugh. (Hey, it might have been the most exciting thing that happened to her that week outside of the seniors' home.) I, however, didn't share her sentiment. In that moment, I needed my own positive perspective, as I could feel my blood beginning to boil. This time, it seemed that "Richard" was the clown, and I was about to become the loose cannon!

"Richard" had so much potential, but he had let me down—big time. I took a moment in our equipment room so I could compose myself and find the words to say. As I stood there, the rhythmic whirring of the compressors and electric motors helped calm me down. Resisting the urge to show "Richard" my anger, I called him into the equipment room and began a serious talk.

I told him what I had just seen. I had seen a young man make an error in judgement that let the team and me down. Then I provided him with a positive perspective like Mr. Strickland would have done with his class clown of '99. I reminded him of all he had done so well recently. This included being a key player in breaking weekly and monthly car wash records. I let him know that I had depended on him during these times and saw him as a leader. I explained that I expected much more from him because he was capable of it and he had demonstrated it many times in the past. The last thing I did (again, as Mr. Strickland would have) was give him time and space. I ordered him to go home early. Since the whole issue began with his frustration about his hours, I told him I would pay him for the rest of his shift, but he had to make one promise to me. He had to promise that he would go fishing (his favourite pastime) and use the time to think about how he would feel if some kid mooned his grandmother.

When "Richard" came into the car wash the next day, I wanted to make sure that things would start to change for the better. I wanted to reinforce what I hoped he had learned the day before. So I asked him a single question: "Are your pants comfortable?"

Confused, he looked at me and said, "I guess so. Why?"

With a smile, I replied, "Good. We're going to be busy today. I want you to keep them up because I can't afford to pay you to fish anymore!"

His smile showed me his perspective had changed, and it became a little more positive.

Stay Connected

Beyond his knack for positive perspectives, Mr. Strickland was a master at staying connected with his students. The best example of this began in the first week of my grade eight classes. Our first task in Mr. Strickland's class was to create and decorate a folder. He explained that this folder was going to house some assignments we would complete throughout the year. The folder was to be our time capsule. Mr. Strickland gave his word that he would deliver our completed time capsules to us in four years' time, when we were to graduate high school. During the next four years, although I had forgotten what exactly was in my personal time capsule, I did wonder if he would actually track me down and deliver it or if he would forget all about it. Only time would tell.

My high school years seemed to go by in the blink of an eye. I had classes during the day, and I worked at the car wash in the evenings and weekends. Before I knew it, I was days away from graduation. It was during my very last day of classes that I was called down to the principal's office. For most students, such a call means bad news, but for the student council president, I assumed final presidential duties awaited me. Instead, I found Mr. Strickland waiting for me with a big smile on his face. In his hand was the folder I had created years earlier. He had kept his promise and even made a personal delivery. In addition to the time capsule, he included a personal letter detailing what he had been up to in the past four years and his contact information should I want to reach out to him with my own update.

Mr. Strickland proved to be a man of his word. He showed me that we can maintain connections and relationships by having a plan and being mindful and deliberate. He hadn't forgotten about his class of 2000, and he once again showed that his students mattered to him. How could I ever forget a teacher like him? I knew that if I ever needed anything, Mr. Strickland was a person I could call upon.

We should all strive to emulate Mr. Strickland's example when developing and maintaining relationships with customers. Building relationships to a point of making strong personal connections requires you to follow through on your promises and remind your customers that they're not forgotten. Fervent loyalty based on personal connections is a loyalty that is very difficult to break. Like Mr. Strickland, stay connected.

When Draj and I were developing our customer

service project, we often discussed the word *personal.* What does it mean? Where does it fit in today's service experiences? The price-conscious and product-savvy consumer of the Information Age has become more demanding than ever while being much less forgiving. The bright screens, both big and small, that incessantly feed us with information have caused a lot of instability as far as good old-fashioned loyalty is concerned. A history of doing business and a firm handshake are no longer enough to keep a customer coming back for more. Today, with the Internet at their fingertips wherever they go, your customers have quick, accurate, and accessible ways of learning how your competitors would suit them.

By the time Draj and I began work on our project, it had been fifteen years since Mr. Strickland first connected with me. Draj and I had set out to meet experts across different industries to provide insights for our customer service program and this book. When Draj asked me who has had an impact on my own life, I didn't need to type the question into Google or ask Siri for the answer. The answer was the first person who popped into my mind: Mr. Strickland. We all know the power of a word-of-mouth referral. If I were to recommend the best grade eight teacher for your child, even to this day I would recommend Mr. Strickland. When it comes to deciding on a product or service, consumers are influenced by what they are invested in emotionally. Consumers who are emotionally invested in products and services will recommend them to everyone they know.

People who build personal relationships build emotional equity. They become the Mr. Stricklands of the business world. How thrilling would it be for your business to be thought of in the same way I think of Mr. Strickland?

The Banker

The first step in creating a mindful experience with a student, customer, or family member is to establish a personal connection. How you do it depends on the circumstances and the individuals involved. In the business world, a common cliché we hear is "it's not personal, it's just business," and that couldn't be further from the truth. It is always personal, and forward-thinking organizations have come to realize that. *Empathy* and *behavioural economics* have replaced *value added* and *re-engineering* as some of the new business buzzwords. Businesses are investing in customer-centric loyalty programs in an effort to stay connected and improve the service experience. The lens has refocused on customer relationships in the battle for market share. The smart companies are the ones striving to ensure that every touchpoint aligns with the ultimate goal of providing an exceptional customer experience that grows and retains relationships. Satisfaction, as previously mentioned, is no longer enough. It's going to take more than that to attract and retain customers and grow the business.

When Jesse and I started working together and

began our own personal connection, we got to talking about past school experiences and teachers. He mentioned a Mr. Strickland right away, a teacher in whose classroom he had sat over fifteen years ago. I considered the impact that Mr. Strickland must have had, as Jesse's face just lit up talking about him as though it was yesterday. So it was no surprise to me that he would want to interview Mr. Strickland for the projects we were developing. I just had to meet my co-worker's hero. Jesse arranged a meeting.

After work one beautiful spring day, I got to meet the famous Mr. Strickland at our local Starbucks. I was running late, so Jesse went ahead without me. I arrived about ten minutes later, and I immediately spotted Jesse with someone who appeared to be one of his twentysomething friends. It wasn't. It was Mr. Strickland! For some reason, I had expected someone older-looking and not quite so…shall I say cool? I found it hard to believe that he had been teaching for almost twenty years.

As we engaged and asked the questions Jesse and I had thoughtfully prepared, I could see and feel the personal connection that Jesse and Mr. Strickland had. Aside from being an excellent conversationalist, Mr. Strickland had a certain genuine humility. One could not help but be drawn to him. We talked about many things, and by the time we said goodbye, I knew why this teacher was so memorable to Jesse. Mr. Strickland is passionate about his life's work and the lives that he feels so privileged to touch. I loved that he readily admitted to continuing the process of learning to be a better teacher and changing his perspective over the years.

As I drove home that day, the experience of meeting and talking with Mr. Strickland triggered a long-forgotten memory. I too had a "Mr. Strickland," but I hadn't realized it until meeting Jesse's. There is a saying about how people come into your life: for a season or a reason. Such was the case with my grade four teacher, Ms. J.

Before reaching grade four, I had been a C student struggling with the English language. I was just getting by. I was the shy one who sat at the back of the classroom. I had a quiet smile and a strange name. "Dragica Turajlic," while beautiful in my native Serbian, was quite the mouthful in English. The first day of school was always entertaining when attendance was called for the first time and my name came up. I remember that school had just started, and on an unseasonably warm autumn day in late September, Ms. J. asked me if I would stay after school. I knew I hadn't done anything wrong, but I fretted about it. I wondered what was going on, and I kept glancing at the clock, yearning for the bell to ring so I could find out.

The reason was soon revealed when I stood before Ms. J. after school. I don't know if it was the glow of autumn sunshine cascading through the windows behind her, but I swear that my teacher at that moment looked like an angel smiling at me. Despite my worst fears, she proceeded to talk to me about *me*. She wanted to know everything about me, and I even learned about her too. She asked me about my parents, my little brother, and even my grandparents, with whom we lived. We talked about cabbage rolls, strudel, and my father's homemade wine and how I helped pick the grapes clean in the basement every year. I told her how I loved to read books, comics, and all sorts of stories and why it took me so long to finish them. I told her that my parents were still learning to speak English too and that I was the one they usually called upon to help them and my grandparents translate. It was a lot of responsibility for a nine-year-old. Perhaps that was one of the reasons why I was serious beyond my years.

That day, Ms. J. asked me if I would help her create a puppet show. A puppet show! And she wanted *me*: *my* voice, *my* personality, and *my* hands to make the puppets come to life. I liked this teacher. I felt so special because she had a personal interest in me and we made a connection. Little did I know that seeds of confidence had been planted that would grow throughout my entire life. She inspired me to become an A student that year and in all the years that followed.

Mr. Strickland and Ms. J., two different teachers from two different eras, both used their special gift of connecting with their students on a personal level by sharing their stories, focusing on the positive perspective (there is always one), and staying connected in whatever way is ideal.

Being mindful of the power of personal connections is essential to providing exceptional customer service and building strong loyalty. Making personal connections can be a game-changer. Being present and genuinely interested in your customers and employees will build these personal connections. This is something that organizations should practice on every level.

Chapter Summary:
The Personal Connection

Share Your Story

- Be both interested and interesting
- Reveal what's important
- Find common ground
- You're more interesting than you think

A Positive Perspective

- Focus on what's going right
- Highlight and build on past achievements
- Put things into perspective
- Give time and space to regroup

Stay Connected

- Have a roadmap
- Set reminders
- Make the effort to follow up
- Take the time to follow through

From mindless to mindful....

When was the last time you called up an old friend or colleague?

Chapter 9

Fix the Feelings

The Banker

Customers are customers, and service is service. The same customer service rules apply whether you're staying at the Ritz-Carlton, getting your car detailed, or applying for a loan. Today, service experiences are compared across different sectors and industries. Even hospitals are now focused on service quality, as they view the patient experience as important for promoting healing and positivity.

Savvy customer-centric companies know they must find ways to differentiate themselves from their competition. As products become increasingly commoditized and easily replicated, service experience is quickly becoming the main differentiator.

While the overall experience can drive differentiation, what happens when things don't go as planned? Worse than that, what happens when things go *completely wrong*? It happens to all of us sooner or later, but if you're lucky, your customer will complain. (If you're not so lucky, silent attrition will be your punishment.) How a company responds to customer complaints and re-solves problems has a direct impact on satisfaction and reputation. Being effective in recovering from a bad sit-uation has the power to actually build customer loyalty and advocacy. Critical to the process is ensuring that you address the emotional aspect of complaints with empathy and genuine sincerity.

Jesse and I discussed at length how to illustrate the art of handling customer complaints for our service program. We recognize that there are well-established best practices readily available. Courses, consultants, and workshops, including the Disney one that Jesse and I attended, are in abundance. There are some great pro-grams being created, and the quest to become "leg-endary" or "world class" in handling customer service issues is in full gear. The organizations that that do well in this respect know how to tell their story and how to leverage their successes. For example, the Ritz-Carlton is renowned for their guest service model: "We are Ladies and Gentlemen serving Ladies and Gentlemen." At Subway, it's not simply a food service employee who makes your sandwich; it's a "Sandwich Artist."

We each had collected lots of stories about com-plaints and concerns that arose at both the bank and the car wash. Today, in our current roles, we work to-gether to respond to and resolve concerns in both sales and service. What we do may not be that much different from any other service-focused organization, but we be-lieve our difference is in the how and the personal way in which we approach each individual we encounter. We call it "fix the feelings." As our guiding principle, it aptly describes an important aspect of our approach and focus.

Perception Is Reality

Whenever a customer expresses a concern or communicates their dissatisfaction, it's an opportunity to alter the course of the relationship and the overall experience. You might think it's a small issue or big one, but it doesn't matter what you think. All that matters is what your customer thinks. Their perception is your reality.

Let's take personalized cheques for example. Believe it or not, people used to write a lot more cheques years ago than they do today. When I started working at the bank, our customers did "in line" banking. Yes, everyone actually came into the branch and stood in line to wait for a teller. Online banking was probably still just an idea in some whiz kid's head. Unless you wanted to carry wads of cash with you all the time, writing a cheque was the primary way to move funds around and pay your rent and your bills.

Ordering cheques was therefore a fairly common occurrence, and it was a manual process just like much of banking. (The computer age was just dawning at the time.) Great care was taken to ensure that all the details were correct before the bank sent the order to the supplier to print. Unfortunately, misprints and errors were bound to happen. Perhaps a name was misspelled or a telephone number had an incorrect digit. Sometimes customers would receive the wrong colour or style. Maybe they'd get green backgrounds instead of blue, flowers instead of scenery, Romalian typeface instead of Helvetica. Whatever the error or issue, customers would let us know. Most did so calmly, and we would simply reorder the cheques. However, for whatever reason, there were usually a handful of customers in each branch who took it as a personal affront. They took it as if we did it on purpose just to bug them.

Now, there's a way to complain and there's a way not to complain. Yelling at a service provider over something easily resolved might be a great way to relieve your own stress, but it's not exactly the best approach. In fact, unless there's some kind of emergency, yelling isn't a good idea. So why would something so seemingly small evoke such an emotional response in some people? I'm reminded of the old adage "the straw that broke the camel's back." Perhaps a cheque order with incorrect spelling was that proverbial last straw that released the floodgates for such an emotional reaction. It doesn't really matter. What matters is to understand that the customer's perception is their reality—that's how they see their world. Who made the error and how it happened is now irrelevant because when the customer's perception becomes their reality, it becomes yours too. Your job is to fix the problem and, more important, the feelings associated with it.

When an issue becomes so personal, you must be

mindful of the emotional aspect of the interaction. I will admit to making my own missteps early in my career. For example, I thought that getting upset because your cheques had dogs on them instead of cats was just plain stupid. Hey, I was a twentysomething whose idea of empathy was still in development. So when I gently suggested to a customer to just use the dog cheques (what was the big deal?), the claws came out (metaphorically, thankfully), and I quickly learned that that was the absolutely wrong thing to say to a cat person!

When dealing with an irate customer, it's always a good idea to take a deep breath before responding. I know all too well what can happen if you don't. I recall sitting in my office near the teller wickets on day while one of my staff was speaking to a man who was visibly upset about something. I edged closer, and I narrowed my focus to see if there was something I could do. I thought maybe I could help diffuse the situation or at least get him into an office to sit down and discuss it. As much as she tried to calm him down and address his feelings, it was a no-win situation. He wasn't moving and he *wasn't* happy. Unfortunately, he just kept raising his voice, louder and louder, until he finally lost it and said quite loudly, "*Look, lady, why don't you just suck my dick!*" Yep, he was quite the class act with those words.

I moved quickly to help her out. I sprung out of my chair and into action, but before I could reach them, she reacted in jaw-dropping fashion. Without pausing or taking a deep breath to calm herself down, she didn't miss a beat. She struck right back, saying, "Well, sir, if you would like to pull down your pants, I will see what I can do."

Oh my. The look on his face was priceless. He was so surprised that he didn't know what to do or say. He quickly fled without uttering another word. I think he must have felt a bit embarrassed. Good. Thankfully, it was near closing time on a Friday, so there were only a few other customers and staff in the branch who heard the very entertaining exchange. While you won't find this story in a best practices workbook on how to handle irate customers, it's here as a reminder that dealing with the public can be difficult. Not everyone is courteous and respectful. Some can be just plain awful, making it nearly impossible for anyone to demonstrate empathy for their perceived reality.

It takes time to develop a thick skin, but it's often difficult to avoid taking things personally regardless. And we sometimes have to recognize that it might not be wise to attempt to "fix the feelings" when someone is too overwrought to maintain any semblance of rational thought. This is an especially important point for those just starting out in their careers. My advice to the rookies: Try not to take it personally, stay calm, and don't forget to breathe!

So how did the story of this no-win situation end? I ended up coaching this staff member on what she could do differently (and hopefully less colourfully) the next time she found herself in a similar situation. I crossed my fingers in my hopes that this type of emotional outburst from customers would be the exception and not the rule. We were both just starting off in our banking careers, and if this was any indication of what lay ahead, we were in for quite a ride!

She thanked me for my support and understanding. As I walked away, I knew it would be something I would not soon forget. Almost thirty years later, it still makes me shake my head and smile.

Show You Care

One of my own personal experiences during my banking life where I required some "fixing the feelings" didn't take place in a bank but in a hospital. In 2011, I found myself in the hospital with a broken leg. However, the story of how I ended up there began a week earlier in Italy. You see, I had been on vacation, hiking along the Amalfi Coast. One of the walks, aptly named *Il Sentiero degli Dei* (The Path of the Gods), is a popular awe-inspiring hiking adventure between the towns of Positano, Praiano, and Agerola. It's a spectacular trek that takes you up to an average height of about 500 metres above the coastline. It's both breathtaking and memorable. So were the million steps I must have climbed in Positano. I remember being so proud of myself going up and down the very steep and narrow passageways filled with all kinds of tripping hazards. I did it all without incident.

Rome was a weekend stopover before the flight home. On the last day, while on a sightseeing jaunt by the entrance to the Coliseum, I spied a street vendor selling an assortment of straw hats. I thought, why not? A hat from Italy to take home. I tried several on and found the perfect one. It was fairly lightweight and tightly woven, and it had a broad brim and was accessorized with a bold leopard-print ribbon. I loved it.

On my first day back at work, I found out that I was asked to attend a company golf tournament at the end of the week. When Friday arrived, I was all ready to go, and at the last minute I remembered my new hat from Italy! I grabbed it, put it on, and looked at myself in the hall mirror for a minute. *Che bellisima!* But in typical fashion, I changed my mind and put it down. With my hand on the doorknob, I was about to leave, but I hesitated, turned to my right, and grabbed the hat and put it back on. Again, I looked in the mirror, but this time it stayed. I turned and headed out, unaware that my split-second decision to wear the hat was going to have a profound impact on the rest of my life.

Well, now you're probably wondering where this story is going. But I know Jesse was totally captivated the first time I told it to him. In fact, most people are once I tell them what happened on the tenth fairway. I was riding shotgun in a golf cart, and as we were going at a good clip, the wind picked up and blew the hat off my head! As I turned to the right to catch it, I howled, "*My hat!*"

Rather than stopping the golf cart, my driver swerved sharply to the left. That motion threw me from the vehicle. I went flying. It happened so quickly, yet it felt like an eternity (almost slow motion) as I floated through the air before landing on the grass. When I heard the snapping of my bones, I knew I was in trouble.

I'm convinced that I made history that day by ending up further into the rough than anyone ever had on that tenth fairway. And rough is an understatement considering how I felt sitting in the emergency room of the Hamilton General Hospital waiting for surgery. That damn hat.

I don't know what was more painful: my broken leg or having to explain to the medical staff and my family what had happened. "You broke your leg playing *golf?*" I could sense the disbelief and a hint of amusement in their voices

I wasn't drinking, nor were we joyriding. It was simply an accident. I survived the treacherous heights of *Il Sentiero degli Dei* only to bust my leg on a golf course.

I felt like such a loser.

That was until I met Dr. Dale Williams, the orthopaedic surgeon who was to perform my surgery. By then, I was a mess. I was worn out from the painkillers, so I was indecisive about the anesthesia and was convinced that I would be one of those statistics who don't wake up after surgery. I couldn't make up my mind on whether I should be half awake or out cold. My son Michael and his wonderful best friend Jesse were with me when Dr. Williams walked in. He had a great smile, has a friendly and folksy voice (I would later learn that he was born and raised in the Maritimes), and he looked right into my eyes when he spoke with me. I may have been in a drug-induced state, but I remember thinking, "Whoa! He looks like Matthew McConaughey." I liked this doctor.

Dr. Williams took the time to deal with my fragile emotional state. He understood that first and foremost he had to fix my feelings before fixing my leg. His approach was never rushed, and he listened to me and asked me all sorts of questions. I believe we established a personal connection. With his assistance, I was able to make up my mind about what to do, and I felt confident that he truly cared about me. I may have been one of many patients that day, but he made me feel like I was the only one.

The operation was a success, and I was fortunate enough to have him continue to look after me for the next eighteen months as I healed. When a second operation was required and I learned that he was going to be away for several months, I decided to wait just for him. When I discovered that his leave of absence was for the birth of his second daughter and for being at home with his family, there was no question as to who should operate on me. Here was an insanely busy surgeon who would talk to you for as long as you needed and answer all your questions. On top of that, he also managed to show that he was a warm and genuine human being.

My leg eventually got better. What happened, happened. I could have moped around and been depressed about it, or I could have mindfully looked for the silver lining in my cloud. It could have been much worse. I needed to shift my perspective to gain a new reality. I know Dr. Williams contributed to that mind shift and helped "fix my feelings." It's with admiration for him that I tell this story. He serves as a great role model. He proves that one can be a brilliant and successful professional and still be a decent human being. A finer doctor I have not met.

Show Them…Again

We've been discussing the importance of putting yourself in your customers' shoes. This is essential if you wish to demonstrate empathy and care. It will certainly contribute to "fixing the feelings" and will move you towards resolving issues. This is all well and good, but is it enough in the high-stakes game of service differentiation? Customer-focused organizations know that they have to do it quicker and better than their competitors. They also give attention to unexpected extras.

Unexpected extras and using the element of surprise become the memorable stories you'll find highlighted in books on customer service. I often tell examples of these stories when facilitating workshops on service. Stories have a life of their own, which is why people tend to remember them better than facts and figures. I don't think I've ever heard someone say to me, "Wow! That bar graph really inspired me." People love hearing stories about other people's experiences, inspirations, and motivational sparks. Sure, there might be facts and figures interwoven in these stories, but storytelling is usually about conveying an important message or lesson.

One of my favourite customer service stories is about a little boy who was with his parents on a Disney Cruise Line ship. The family was at dinner, and the boy wasn't having a great day even though it was the first day of their trip.

When the waiter asked him what he wanted for dessert, the boy quietly looked up, whispered, "Nothing," and hung his little head down again. So the waiter decided to give the boy exactly what he wanted. He returned with a plate upon which the word *nothing* was written in chocolate sauce. Yes, this is the stuff of legend, of Disney magic. Their employees are trained in and focused on finding those magical moments. But what stops others from being just as mindful? How do we thoughtfully look for ways to show we care? Not just once but over and over again!

In my experience, I've found that if you just pause and think about what would make the ordinary into something special or extraordinary, the light bulb will go off! When dealing with customer complaints, we are too often focused on solving the problem quickly that we don't focus on solving the problem *effectively*. Even I have been guilty of that. When a customer would call, frantic about something or other, I would often solve the issue and then move on to the next problem. Rarely would I ever follow up. After all, the issue was resolved in my books.

I later discovered that we can purposefully create lasting impressions by simply taking the interaction one step further. I'm referring to making it a priority, after the problem is resolved, to follow up with customers in ways that are appropriate to each situation. Showing them you care enough to take the time to do this, no matter how small a gesture, could be memorable. It can be a simple phone call or, better yet, a handwritten note accompanied with a small token of appreciation. Jesse and I have often received heartfelt thank-you calls and emails from the customers we have followed up with in this manner. If these customers are willing to go out of their way to thank us for this, just imagine what they're telling their friends, family, co-workers, etc.

The Kid

Washing someone's car is usually much less emotional than dealing with someone's life savings in a bank or treating them in a hospital. Or so I thought. There was one very sensitive situation that always sticks out in my memory. It happened during my early days at the car wash.

Imagine this scenario. You've just spent $208,000 on a brand new Porsche 911 Turbo S. Yep, that's right; you spent four and a half times the average annual salary and more than double the RRSP holdings of the average Canadian on a single car! But at least it's one very beautiful car. Congratulations! Naturally, you want to keep this car in pristine shape and keep it clean. Now imagine that you left your brand new Porsche that you worked very hard to pay for in the capable hands of your trusted local car wash. When the car comes out, it's clean and shiny, except you notice that on the driver's side both the front and rear wheels look like they picked a fight with a jackhammer. When I saw this situation unfold right in front of my eyes, I might have been only seventeen years old. I was unprepared for the customer's reaction: the look of horror on his face morphed into rage.

Thankfully and fortunately for me, Claudio, the car wash owner, was standing right beside me as the Porsche rolled out. This wasn't something as simple as an incorrect font or graphic on a box of cheques, nor was it a minor service issue; this was a major problem. In both the customer's perception *and* in reality. Claudio quickly and calmly sprung into action. Through his actions, he showed that he was genuinely concerned about what had happened. The scratched rims were the result of a perfect storm: a new car that had not been tested through the car wash, an employee sending it through the wash without checking the width of the wheels, and the steering wheel turned ever so slightly to the left causing the wheels to rub up against the steel track guiding the car. It was very clear that the car wash would have to pay for the wheel repairs and also provide a rental car to our customer while his car was in the shop.

Watching Claudio handle the situation, the way he calmed and reassured the customer, was a good lesson for me, and it was an experience that served me well once I became the car wash manager. Above all else, put yourself in the customer's shoes. Claudio demonstrated the empathy that the customer needed to see and feel.

True enough, major incidents like this were rare at the car wash, but we also had our fair share of smaller service complaints, which were just as important. No matter how capable you or your team is, mistakes will happen. There will be errors, and someone will inevitably drop the ball. The challenging part is when you have customers who don't openly display their emotions—right there and then. How can you make things right with customers who quietly seethe about something that's gone wrong? When they leave never to return, you've missed an opportunity to build trust and loyalty. What's worse is they may spread bad word of mouth. This is unfortunate because you didn't even get a chance to show you care. Those who excel at delivering great service experiences constantly pay attention and pick up on cues, both verbal and non-verbal. Try not to miss opportunities to make things right.

The way the customer perceives the situation needs to become your reality. Being keenly aware of how certain issues make people feel will help you in addressing the issues and in following up later. This is how you retain customers and build a loyal customer base.

So after I became the manager of the car wash, I would be responsible for resolving issues and "fixing the feelings" of our customers. I tried doing what Claudio would do as I had witnessed him in the past. It was a case of a lot of the little issues going unnoticed until they added up to one big problem. The first example of which started with a simple dent in a license plate.

A panicked employee barged into my office to tell me about a poor senior who had accidentally backed her car into a parked BMW that was behind her in line. The customer with the BMW had left his car in line so that the staff could prepare it. He had paid for his car wash and was waiting for his car to be finished. Fortunately, the collision was very minor. The only damage to the BMW was a slightly scratched and bent license plate. When I went to break the news to the owner of the BMW, he was quite relieved that the damage wasn't worse, though he was unimpressed with the state of his license plate. It wasn't the car wash's fault, but it had happened on our property. What I did next surprised both the employee who barged into my office and the customer with the BMW.

I gave the customer the amount of money it would cost for replacement license plates on his car even though it wasn't our fault that another customer backed into his car. We needed to show that we cared about his experience and business with the car wash. In addition to paying for the license plates, I also gave him two complimentary car wash coupons that he could use on subsequent visits, and I assured him that these types of incidents weren't the norm at our car wash. The customer was very happy. He was surprised at how far we went to "fix his feelings" and the issue. When his two complimentary car wash coupons were used up, the first thing he did was buy a booklet of ten more.

Picking up on the little things, should they be your fault or not, and making your customer feel valued enough that you take action may turn a dissatisfied customer you may never see again into a loyal supporter. In the case of the customer with the BMW, a small unexpected gesture not only saved the day, it strengthened the customer's relationship with the car wash beyond what it would have been if the accident hadn't happened in the first place. Why would he trust any other car wash after what we did for him? Why not keep going to the car wash that would take care of him again in the future?

Progressive organizations that pay attention to the human aspect of complaints and are mindful about their customers' feelings are the organizations that will grow and prosper with the help of their legions of loyal customers.

Chapter Summary:
Fix the Feelings

Perception Is Reality

- Your customer's perception is *your* reality
- Put yourself in your customers' shoes
- Adjust your own lens

Show You Care

- Take the time
- Fix the feelings
- Empathize and relate—state why the complaint is important to *you*

Show Them…Again

- People remember stories, not data—give them personal stories worth remembering
- Set a reminder to follow up after a complaint has been resolved
- Create a lasting impression

From mindless to mindful….

What story do you want your customers to tell about you?

Chapter 10

A Reason to Remember

The Kid

Have you ever experienced that awkward situation where a familiar face greets you and you can't remember their name? You likely muster a few words like "Oh hello! How are you?" in a pleasantly surprised tone as though you know exactly who they are. Hoping your thespianism buys you time, you then attempt to move the conversation forward to spark a memory of the person's name. In most cases, the attempt is a fool's errand, ultimately resulting in an admission that you're "horrible at remembering names."

Why is it that we can remember plenty of useless facts and trivia but draw a blank when it comes to remembering such an important detail like someone's name? Richard Harris, a professor of psychology at Kansas State University, will tell you that it's not your memory that you should blame but rather your interest level in the person:

"Almost everybody has a good memory for something," Harris said.

The key to a good memory is your level of interest, he said. The more interest you show in a topic, the more likely it will imprint itself on your brain. [...][3]

Being mindful of this advice will not only help you remember someone's name, it can also serve you well in building a relationship with them. You may be pleasantly surprised at what you will learn by paying attention to even the subtleties of what they tell you. Be interested.

Today, differentiation of product and price is diminishing, and choice is in abundance. Organizations are finding it increasingly difficult to create enough interest to imprint themselves on their customers' brains. Reduced differentiation can be attributed to the increase in savvy Internet-connected consumers. Savvy customers have greater expectations and constantly force organizations to raise the bar of value and innovation. This puts pressure on organizations to compete like mad within their respective industries, leading to a kind of market "arms race." Many organizations have become so focused on this arms race that they haven't observed their more successful peers. The successful organizations have a better understanding of their customers, and they delight them with the unexpected. They show their appreciation by taking an individual approach with their customers. This focused approach gives customers a very good reason to remember their experiences. Sometimes the approach has customers remembering exceptional employees by name, just like "Charlie" from the Apple Store, who is discussed in Chapter 3.

While the Apple Store may have had "Charlie," the car wash had the incomparable Ronnie, whose name will forever be imprinted on my brain thanks to everything he taught me. Those who know him will agree wholeheartedly that he is an incredibly special person. It's the perfect way to describe him. Ronnie stood well over six feet and had a handlebar moustache, and he was a full fifty-four years older than our youngest employee. Although he looked different from the rest of us, it wasn't his distinctive and uncommon look that made him stand out; it was his mindful approach to his customers. He was intent on creating memorable experiences and giving customers a reason to remember that car wash right beside the little grocery market. The car wash wasn't just a place to wash your car when Ronnie was in the house; it was a show, and Ronnie was the star.

Whistle While You Work

Every customer who came to the car wash had one thing in common: They had a dirty car and wanted to pay us to clean it. We could do that, but so could the other full-service car wash in the city. The similarities between us and our competition across town weren't a secret. We had the same layout, similar cleaning equipment, and similar prices. In addition, we had to compete with the twelve touchless car washes in the city.

Failing to give our customers a reason to remember us would mean that their decision to return would be based solely on location and convenience. It's generally accepted in the car wash industry that your volume of customers will be 0.5 percent of the number of cars that drive past your location each day. It's no secret, then, that whoever has more drive-by traffic has more dollars in the cash register. So what made us an outlier? Why did customers drive further to get their car washed with us rather than the competition? How did we double our industry average? Fortunately, what made us different from the competition wasn't a secret either. The differentiating factor was our people—including Ronnie, who was at the heart of it all. We gave customers a reason to remember us. Location and convenience gave way to destination and adventure.

A memorable experience is often created by something new, something we've never seen or heard before—a surprise. Ronnie played a starring role in surprising and delighting our customers. Although he was one of the last employees that customers would interact with as he put the finishing touches on their cars, they could hear him from one end of the car wash tunnel to the other.

While growing up in the harsh reality of postwar Germany, Ronnie yearned to play a musical instrument.

His mother, a widow raising nine children, couldn't afford to give him an instrument. Instead of being weighed down by disappointment, he listened to his mother's advice to look into his heart and develop his musical talents from within. So Ronnie became a gifted whistler and an entertaining singer. Thanks to years of practice, he wasn't afraid to share his musical talents along with his car washing talents.

As customers waited for their cars, Ronnie would delight them with a serenade, something they would have never expected at a car wash. Where else could you get serenaded at a car wash? Certainly not across town.

Ronnie would also give our customers the lay of the land. While pretending to look serious and stern, he would make sure everyone knew that "Pregnant ladies come first, then the kids. Everyone else comes next, and people with bad attitudes go to the back of the line!" This made both the children and the adults laugh each time. Parents would appreciate the attention Ronnie gave to their laughing kids. And Ronnie loved to joke with the children. He would continue his routine of being this stern yet silly character by saying, "You think this is funny? There will be no laughing here—this is serious business!" and daring the children to laugh with a twinkle in his eye. The more he challenged them, the more they would laugh.

Children loved coming into the car wash. Their curious young eyes would watch the rainbow-coloured soaps and big spinning brushes clean the family car.

And as if that weren't enough for them, Ronnie was there at the end of the car wash to make everything so much more special. His larger-than-life personality consistently delivered unexpected delight along with a clean car.

Customers who drove away in their nice clean car may have forgotten what type of car wash they got by the time they left the parking lot, but they most definitely remembered their unexpected experience thanks to Ronnie.

Make It Yours

If Ronnie was the star of every interaction with customers, then the customers were unquestionably the unexpected co-stars. Ronnie always brought them into the act and included them in the experience. They felt special and important because he tailored his approach to each one. For instance, if he noticed an Italian flag sticker on the bumper of a car, he would begin to sing and converse to the customer in Italian. If he found out that it was a customer's birthday, he would whistle "Happy Birthday" and invite everyone in the car wash to join in. If a customer appeared shy, he wouldn't make them uncomfortable by putting them in the spotlight, but he would still perform so the customer could still observe him and still drive away entertained. Such were Ronnie's personal touches.

Ronnie was always mindful of who his customers were so he could deliver what they needed. A person with a frown got a smile, a mother with hyperactive children got a break, and seniors got attention and care. As mundane as a car wash is to most people, there would be no forgetting the time you got your car washed while Ronnie whistled and danced just for *you* because he found out it was your birthday.

The key to creating an experience that people will remember is to individualize your approach so your customers know you're mindful of their needs. They need to feel important and appreciated. They *are* important, and they *should* be appreciated. People remember those who appreciate them. Relationships can easily be short-lived for those who take their customers for granted. Customers have choices, and if they can get the same product or service elsewhere—in this case, the same quality car wash—they will choose the place that appreciates them and gives the experience a personal touch.

Point the Passion

The Ronnies of the world take a service transaction and turn it into an experience that people love. If this is as true as I believe it to be when it comes to people, how do we get everyone else to be a little more like Ronnie? The answer is scary: You have to give your people the power to become memorable. If you've hired the right people, it's already in them to do so.

Many organizations, however, provide their front-line employees with scripted greetings or talking points to use in customer interactions. Like the example of the teller in Chapter 2, pointing the passion of your people means letting them go off the company script and find their own voice. Yes, let them go off script—the script that's so aligned with brand and image in the minds of organizational leaders. Scary, isn't it? Providing frontline employees with scripts makes for robotic interactions and makes your organization seem like it's staffed with automatons—a mindless staff repeating the same lines, day in and day out. If you toss out the script, your staff will shed their creative shackles and they will have the freedom they need to create memorable experiences.

Not everyone is a natural entertainer like Ronnie, but they don't have to be. When people are free to be themselves, they can discover their own ways to give customers memorable experiences. Leaders can help their people figure out how to do this by pointing them to their passion.

I was able to do just that with an employee named "Eric" (not his real name), who was a dedicated car enthusiast. He was very intelligent and physically capable, which in theory made him a perfect fit for our car prep and vacuuming position. This position required little interaction with customers, but it was fast paced and physically demanding. It was tough as hell. "Eric" performed well in his duties but was becoming increasingly difficult to motivate, as it was clear he was getting bored. I tried to switch up his duties to give him more variety, and that's when I became more mindful of pointing out people's passion.

"Eric" loved to talk—*a lot*. And what he really loved to talk about was what he was passionate about: cars. I thought some fresh air outside of the car wash and a chance to speak with customers about their pride and joy would be a good fit for him. So I transferred him to our greeter and sales writing position.

Early on, I observed him as he dealt with customers, as I was afraid that his youthful exuberance in addition to his penchant for chattering would get the better of him. I also felt he may have been taking too long to process orders, but my fears were quickly erased. I was wrong. I noticed the customers' broad smiles as they walked into the car wash knowing that their baby would be taken care of. People love their cars, and so did "Eric." The customers knew that someone who admired their car would take the finest care of it. He would remember each person by car and make them feel as special and unique as the car they drove.

Moving "Eric" to a position where his passion was pointed in the right direction was one of the best moves I made at the car wash. "Eric" continued talking about cars even after he left his car wash career ready for a new challenge. He lives his passion through his work every day. He now helps his customers find the perfect car as a successful sales associate. He has many return customers, which is proof that he gives people a reason to remember him.

Giving "Eric" the power to go out and freely interact with customers turned out to be important to the success of the car wash. Between "Eric's" key role as a greeter and sales writer and Ronnie's show as a finale, we created fun memories for the people who chose to drive across town to put their dollars in our cash register—and tip jar.

The Banker

I will always remember meeting Ronnie. It was like Christmas in July—a delightful and memorable surprise.

It was a gorgeous Saturday morning as we headed to the Welland Farmer's Market, where we would find Ronnie in action. Jesse had purposely not given me any prior information about where he would be or even what he looked like. All I knew was that he used to work with Jesse at the car wash and he had a lasting impact on him. Jesse said that he was a master of creating a memorable experience and that the car wash customers loved him. "Hmm. From a car wash to a farmer's market?" I thought. "Is there a difference?" I would soon find out.

We had decided beforehand that I would simply wander the aisles and take in all the sights and sounds. The market is fairly compact with several aisles and two buildings, so I knew it wouldn't take me long to complete my scouting. All the while, Jesse walked by my side with a smile on his face and amusement in his eyes. I stopped at several booths that I thought were possibilities, to see and feel if there was anything special about them that stood out. I ended up purchasing tomatoes, peppers, and a bouquet of freesias. These were friendly and pleasant service experiences, but I knew I hadn't met Ronnie yet. I had to keep going.

It was in the building that housed the meat and cheese vendors where I noticed a commotion halfway down the aisle. A small crowd had gathered, and as Jesse and I edged closer, I could hear a distinctive voice with a German accent talking to the crowd. Well, "talking" doesn't adequately describe what was going on. Judging by the smiles on people's faces and the attention it was garnering, *performing* is a better word to describe it. This was pure entertainment. I turned to find Jesse, but he had left my side. He too had joined the enraptured crowd.

Taking it all in, I knew I had found Ronnie.

The car wash had indeed been exchanged for a stall at the farmer's market. Instead of supporting a team, Ronnie was now a one-man show selling all sorts of homemade sausages and salami. Other vendors were selling similar products, but Ronnie's stall was the one most people stopped at. Perhaps it was his broad grin and friendly greeting that captured people's attention. Whatever it was, people were compelled to stop and speak with him. Maybe it was the way he noticed the children. Like a friendly character in a children's book, or even Santa Claus, the children were drawn to him. With his handlebar moustache and twinkling brown eyes, he would flash them a smile and say something about how special they were. Compliments flowed easily from his lips. There was something magical about him, and the children recognized this instantly.

Ronnie's generosity was also in abundance. After checking with Mom or Dad, he would slice ample pieces of kielbasa for the children. There were no tiny samples skewered with toothpicks on Ronnie's counter. Oh no. Ronnie made sure the samples were as generous as his smile.

Watching this scene unfold numerous times, I didn't know whose reactions were more delightful, Ronnie's or his visitors'. Either way, I wasn't surprised to see that once people were engaged and talking with him they ultimately purchased some of his kielbasa, and his salami too. Nobody left this stall empty-handed. People like to do business with people they like. As much as the car wash customers liked Ronnie, those who visited him at the farmer's market liked him immensely.

Jesse eventually introduced us, and we managed to have a lovely chat in between customers. Ronnie was genuine and sincere, and he made me laugh. I too bought some salami to take home, and I'm a vegetarian!

Jesse was right; Ronnie was special.

Making a lasting impression and giving people a reason to remember you can result from actions both big and small. As a service provider, you may not be aware of the impact of your actions until years later. For me, it was almost two decades later that I discovered by accident what a difference I had made in one young woman's life.

A couple of years ago, one of my managers wanted me to meet a potential new hire. Her name was Justine. My manager gave me a brief summary of the interview and how Justine had answered her interview questions. One of the questions had her describe a service experience and someone who had made a difference. Justine had told her about how she applied for a loan at several banks when she was in her early twenties. They had all turned her down—except one. The manager at one of the banks didn't say no right away. She said she would work on it and do her best to get the deal approved. Justine still remembered her and was always grateful for what the manager did and how she made her feel. I thought that Justine sounded like a promising applicant who valued and appreciated good service.

When I met Justine the next day, she looked at me and said, "We've already met at the Centre Mall, about twenty years ago. You were the one who gave me my loan." I didn't remember her at first, as it was a long time ago, but as she filled in the details, it slowly all came back.

It was a great feeling to know that I had made such a difference in her life, and especially when she needed it the most. She thanked me again, and I thanked her for reminding me that what was true about customer service then is just as true today. When I told her about including this story in the book, she sent me an email thanking me and once again reminded me in her words: "Great customer service lasts a lifetime."

Justine was hired as a part-time teller. She has since proven herself a bright light, and she rose quickly though the ranks. She's now running her own branch, and I have no doubt that she gives everyone she meets a reason to remember her.

Chapter Summary:
A Reason to Remember

Whistle While You Work
- Make it memorable
- Smiles are free—be generous with them
- Laughter is contagious—include staff *and* customers
- Create experiences, not transactions

Make It Yours
- Everyone plays a role—what's yours?
- Co-star with your customer—bring them into the act
- Find thoughtful extra touches

Point the Passion
- Leverage people's talents
- Be open to new ideas
- Be prepared to be surprised
- Don't be afraid to colour outside the lines

From mindless to mindful....

How do you want to be remembered?

Chapter 11

How Can You Mend a Broken Heart?

The Kid

Important question: How can you mend a broken heart? Okay, let's not be so dramatic. You might not exactly have to mend someone's broken heart. That would (I hope) be a very rare case, but you *will* eventually have to re-evaluate the relationship with a customer based upon their experience with you or someone in your organization. And while it's rare that you will break a customer's heart, I've learned that matters of the heart and of customer relationship management require a similar approach with the same level of mindfulness and care. It doesn't matter how good and consistent your service is; nobody's perfect, and mistakes will happen. Those mistakes will sometimes lead you to a new opportunity to re-evaluate the relationship and determine what's working, what isn't, and where the relationship is headed.

In my growth from a fourteen-year-old kid working at a car wash to where I am today, my experiences dealing with difficult customers and situations have taught me important lessons about the dangers of dogmatic thinking. You know those old aphorisms everyone used to quip (and some still do): "the customer is always right," "the customer is king," etc. Well, in my experience, I've learned that those sayings are wrong. You don't *always* have to mend a broken heart or a customer relationship.

Don't get me wrong. I wish those sayings were true. If they were, customer service would be easy; your customers would simply communicate everything they want, and you would mindlessly do whatever they say. It was challenging for me to understand this early on in my career, as I accepted such aphorisms with dogmatic thinking. As a result, I couldn't figure out how to effectively manage customers who tried to take advantage of my naïveté.

The problem is that customer relationships can be like personal relationships in that most people are good and honest, but some can be downright deceitful and malicious, seeking their own benefit with little regard for others. A "what's in it for me?" attitude of the relatively few absolutely ruins the idea that the customer is always right. I eventually learned that it's similar to dating: If things aren't working out, it's okay to say no, and sometimes it might be for the best to part ways.

So You're Breaking Up with Me?

My first breakup with a customer came early in my management career at the car wash. It was a beautiful late summer day, and the sun was shining on the row of dirty cars lined up outside the car wash. Things were running smoothly, and I was starting to daydream about the end of the day, when I could jump on my motorcycle and take an evening ride along the lake. Ah, the rumble of the engine helping me unwind from a long day—the warm breeze on my face and the setting sun reflecting off the water making me feel like the moment could last forever....

"Jesse...! *Jesse*...?" My daydream was immediately interrupted as "Tiffany" (not her real name), one of our youngest and newest employees, had shouted my name. She looked very concerned. It was her first job, and she was only a few weeks into her employment. "You looked like you were really focused on something," she said. "I'm sorry to bother you."

I assured her that it was okay and urged her to continue. She explained that there was a customer who insisted on driving his truck onto the car wash conveyor, but he didn't want to stay in his truck while it travelled through the wash. She had told him that for safety reasons he would have to remain in the vehicle or let one of the attendants drive his truck onto the conveyor system. He was insistent and quite pushy, causing "Tiffany" to panic. "Tiffany" was a very sweet girl, but she was inexperienced, so she was at loss as to what to do and say to this customer. I told her not to worry and to wait in my office while I went out and spoke with him.

I exited my office, and just as I rounded the corner towards the entry of the car wash, I saw a full-sized GMC truck come barrelling out of the tunnel in reverse, nearly striking two employees who were passing by. As the truck was in motion, its owner, a very short man with a small frame, was able to jump in and push the emergency brake. I thought my heart was going to stop. At that point, I was enraged. He could have hurt or killed someone. But when I recognized him, I knew that the time had come. This last stunt of his was the final straw. This customer and the car wash were going to break up.

Although he was a regular car wash customer, he constantly disregarded safety regulations, and enough was enough. He routinely ignored us when we asked him to stay clear of the work area and machinery. We gave him plenty of warnings that he was endangering his safety and the safety of others in the car wash.

As I approached him, I had expected him to take accountability and apologize. But no. That's not what happened. Instead, he barked at me. "*Stupid* kids! What were they doing standing there? They could have been killed!" The nerve! My blood was now boiling. If I were a teakettle, you would have been able to hear me whistling for miles! *Nobody* speaks about my staff that way, especially not someone who almost hurt two innocent bystanders.

When I asked the man to leave, our conversation wasn't pretty. Just like real breakups, sometimes such conversations are loud and uneasy. The most difficult thing to do when you're breaking up in the professional sense, however, is to avoid taking it personally. The key is to remain as professional as possible.

So maybe now you're wondering if I was very professional with this guy. The answer is no (but I've certainly learned since then), and as bad as it may sound, I can't say I regret it. My people's safety came first.

Not every customer is going to be as obvious to break up with as one who tries to run you over with a truck. The real skill to ending a relationship is doing it with finesse and knowing exactly when it's warranted and appropriate to do so.

Mend It Before It Breaks

When it comes to dealing with matters of the heart on a personal level and customer relationships on a professional level, the best skill to sharpen is the ability to anticipate potential problems before they blow up in your face. I was recently reminded of this while on a trip out to the oldest golf course in North America, where I experienced a (self-inflicted) near breakdown. While Draj and I were developing our projects, I was able to arrange a meeting with the owner and hands-on operator of the Niagara-on-the-Lake Golf Club. It's a beautiful course situated along the shoreline of Lake Ontario, and it has welcomed golfers since 1875. In 1895, it held the very first international tournament on North American soil.

As rich as this course is in history and beauty, it's also steeped in a tradition of service excellence thanks to its owner/operator, John Wiens. John was our last interview for our projects, and fittingly so. Here was a leader who was firing on all cylinders. He talked about how much the customer's first impression matters, making the experience memorable, and, most important, how culture is everything. It all sounded so similar to what the others had already told us. It was exciting to speak with someone who gets it, and I really admired John for his work ethic and his passion for leading by example. But something else happened to me that day that really made the visit special, and it occurred right before my meeting with John.

The seeds of my near breakdown were planted a few weeks before I showed up at the golf course. I had been very unsuccessful in arranging an appointment with John. Our schedules were very hectic, and we had to reschedule many times. When we finalized a date, I knew John was doing me a favour by taking time out of his busy day to meet with me, so the least I could do was be punctual and show up at our agreed-upon time of 10:00 a.m.

I had figured out when to leave for the golf course, and I even added in some extra time so I wouldn't be late. To my horror, I failed to anticipate the movable bridge I had to cross that just happened to be raised to let a freight ship pass through. I found myself stuck in my car, and the clock was ticking. I felt sick to my stomach, thinking I was going to let John down. As the bridge lowered, I put the pedal to the metal, and I finally made it to the golf course. I glanced at my watch: 9:56 a.m. No speeding ticket, and I made it on time…or so I thought. Getting out of my car in what I thought was the parking lot, I quickly realized I was nowhere near the clubhouse. I was in a parking lot for utility vehicles. I was most certainly going to be late. I couldn't even see the clubhouse. So much for my making a good first impression! But something happened that saved the day.

A man who wasn't in a "traditional customer-facing role" (who I would later discover worked on the grounds) noticed me walking around looking panicked. He must have noticed my frantic look because he quickly approached me and simply said, "You look lost. Where are you trying to go?" I explained that I was looking for the clubhouse and that I was going to be late. He pointed me in the right direction, but when he saw me walking towards my car, he went a step further and said, "Hey, you're already late, and you won't get parking anywhere near the clubhouse today. My name is Vic. Why don't you hop in my truck? I'm going to get you there on time." As I thanked Vic and swung his truck door shut, I glanced at my watch: 9:59 a.m. I made it.

Vic didn't have to do what he did. It wasn't in his job description. He was responsible for taking care of the grounds. He had no way of knowing if I was a golfer or not, but he understood that there would be no grounds to maintain if there weren't any happy golfers to use them. He knew that his responsibility was to take care of the course, and that may mean doing things outside of his formal job description. He was observant and thoughtful in his approach, as he anticipated a potential issue with my experience (and my day) and was able to fix it before it broke completely.

Though what Vic did for me may seem so simple, my experience at Niagara-on-the-Lake Golf Course had shades of the best qualities of those I admire: the precision of Apple, the engagement of Ronnie, and the culture of White Oaks. I doubt that this hole-in-one experience could have happened in an organization that lacked the mindful leadership of someone like John and the dedication of his employees.

Chapter Summary:
How Can You Mend a Broken Heart?

So You're Breaking Up with Me?

- Don't tolerate disrespectful behaviour in the workplace—whether from staff or customers
- Don't take it personally
- Weigh the long-term pros and cons
- Don't rush to judgement
- Explain reasoning professionally

Mend It Before It Breaks

- Anticipate problems before they get bigger
- Don't be afraid to actively engage and offer a helping hand
- Take ownership and act decisively

From mindless to mindful....

Are you putting your heart into your work?

Chapter 12

Hearts and Minds

You now know how the paths of the former bank executive and the kid from the car wash converged and how their inspirations drew them to the same conclusions. You have also met some of the people who helped them get there. However, there are a few more details regarding how the two ended up on Bay Street launching their customer service program.

So what about that program? You will remember that it was but an idea on the day they attended the Disney quality service workshop at White Oaks. They were only beginning to roll up their sleeves and figure out what they would do. Once they decided on the "what," the next crucial items were the "how" and the "who." *How* would they go about presenting their ideas? *Who* would be the first to participate and help them fill in the missing pieces? These were the important questions they asked themselves and each other. They each had their doubts. Their internal dialogue nagged them:

"Who are *we* to take on such a grand endeavour?"

"What makes us think *we* can get it done?"

However, the Banker and the Kid knew that fate had thrown them together for a reason. The more they personally connected with each other, the more they discovered just how much they had in common. They knew they didn't know everything, and they didn't pretend to, but one thing they knew for certain was that they shared a passion for creating a customer service program that made sense, one that covered the important stuff that somehow, for whatever reason, gets forgotten. Their respective careers in customer service had prepared them well, and in some ways they knew it was all part of a plan. Perhaps it was the same plan that resulted in their collaboration in the writing of this book.

However, they had underestimated the work that would be required to create their program, so they worked tirelessly to see the program through to completion. It was a good thing they liked each other, as they would banter over the smallest of details—to them, those mattered the most. Once they were committed to the process, their hearts and minds were enthralled. Regardless of the outcome, they were all in.

Although the concept of "winning hearts and minds" originated as a wartime strategy and has been employed in several conflicts over the past century, it's a concept that is trending with popular business minds and leadership gurus. The context here is not about fighting to win battles but about building employee engagement.

What is employee engagement? It may mean something different to each organization, and it may vary across industries, but in the context of the message in this book, it means leveraging the commitment and passion of employees so that they deliver a mindful and delightful service experience to customers. Inspired and empowered employees are willing to do the unexpected extra for their customers. They will do this because they can and, more important, *because they want to*. Through their respective experiences and their shared stories, the Banker and the Kid have learned that the customer experience mirrors the employee experience.

So when they first began discussing ways to engage employees in the creation of a customer service program, the Banker and the Kid were mindful of the need to connect with them both emotionally and intellectually. It was clear that getting buy-in would be easier if those involved in implementation were also given the opportunity to be co-creators. Employees on the frontline know what works and what doesn't work. This wasn't going to be a top-down program. While the framework and outline of key concepts were provided to the branches, there was no mandate for how everything would be communicated and operationalized.

The two pilot teams were asked to provide creative ideas and honest feedback from the official launch party down to the monthly planning and implementation. It was important that they stayed true to their basic tenets. What did the staff need and how could the duo help?

The program needed enough latitude for personalization. After all, the success of the initiative was directly related to and dependent on the employees who would deliver it and bring it to life—individually and as a team. There would be new and different ways of working, and as with all changes, people need an adjustment period to find their way and to get their creative energies flowing. This was about building commitment, not compliance.

All Aboard

Choosing who they thought were the right people with the right attitude was a key first step, and they spent many hours discussing who their "cast members" would be. Walt Disney would be proud to see the energy they expended in making their decisions. Having strong leaders and engaged teams was a non-negotiable. The Banker and the Kid knew that this would determine whether the program succeeded or a flopped. There had to be a healthy balance between the heart and the mind. Yes, the emotional aspect was important; there had to be a natural desire to connect with and help people in addition to a cognitive ability to learn and think on the fly and handle uncertainty.

Above all else, the Banker and the Kid needed everyone on board with 100 percent commitment to the goals of the program.

All Roads Lead to Rome….

Having assembled the two teams for the pilot program,

never was a proverb more suitable for the duo as they embarked on the journey: "All roads lead to Rome." They soon realized something based on what they already knew from their own experiences: The two teams could take different paths and still arrive at the same destination and achieve the same goal. They watched as both teams contributed their own ideas on how to get there.

While it certainly wasn't like "herding cats," they still had to be confident enough to allow for freedom of expression. They knew the importance of empowering employees to put their own signature on their work. The only requirement was to maintain certain components of the program that were foundational. The "how" was entirely up to the employees to create and implement.

The successful implementation of the program was also dependent on genuine leadership. If the leadership in the branches wasn't aligned with the program and didn't "walk the talk," then how the heck could anyone expect people to follow suit? Personalization, then, became a dominant theme. The leaders had to make the employees feel special, and they could only do that by paying attention to the details and taking the time to make it personal. The program's initial welcome kit was personalized for each team member, complete with a personal welcome letter from their leaders. The thoughts and ideas in the letter weren't scripted or prescribed; they were the leadership's genuine thoughts on customer service and what the program would do for the staff and organization.

As expected, each branch followed a different path in implementing the program. It was a welcome approach that provided additional lessons and ideas on what worked and what didn't. The hope was that broad parameters would encourage employees to pick and choose what worked best for their team and their customers. In other words, they would personalize the program for their own branch.

The Banker and the Kid attended and participated in both launches—one in the same small town where the Kid had worked at the car wash, and the other on Bay Street, familiar ground to the Banker. It was delightful but not surprising to see how different the teams were, yet they each communicated the key messages with clarity and consistency. What was most impressive (and memorable) was the energy and enthusiasm each team demonstrated. It was palpable and exciting. They were the right people for the program, and they were on their way.

A Job vs. a Purpose

One of the measures of success was whether those involved in the pilot program began to view their jobs and the roles they played with a sense of purpose. Frontline employees have jobs that are quite transactional, but what is their purpose? How many employees can see beyond their transactional duties and will act like Vic at the golf course or like Ronnie at both the car wash and the farmer's market?

Having a purpose in your work means being mindful of your customers' emotions and understanding how you play a supporting role in them. For example, if you discover that a customer is withdrawing money to cover a funeral expense, comfort them and make the transaction secondary. If a couple is buying their first home, recognize the significance of the milestone and celebrate with them rather than focus so much on the business aspects.

Making a customer experience personal and memorable requires taking responsibility to do so even if it involves others. This is particularly true when service complaints and other problems require the involvement of others to fix the issue. As the first person to speak with the customer, recognize the importance of "fixing the feelings," not only as a job function but as a function of your purpose. Stepping up and taking responsibility regardless of why it happened or who is to blame demonstrates taking ownership of the customer experience.

While many would argue that no one does it better than the folks at Disney, who will go to all sorts of lengths to ensure their guests needs are addressed, the Banker and the Kid would argue that they have found two teams that rival the best that Disney has to offer.

Some Final Words:
Simple Truths

When the program was launched and we began our journey to write this book, we asked ourselves, "Are we being too simple?" Our purpose was to present what we were passionate about, but we knew that some would say our stories and truths were obvious. While this may be the case, knowing something is not the same as embracing it and doing it. For us, knowledge without action is a wasted opportunity. We decided we weren't going to waste ours.

We spent a lot of time sharing our own personal stories with each other first. We knew each other on a professional level, but many a Saturday morning would while away as we told each other about our lives and the people who had an impact on us. We realized just how powerful it was being present and in the moment with each other. We were simultaneously interested in and interesting to each other.

While working on the book, our sense of mindfulness went into high gear. We noticed that we would make references to certain chapters during our day-to-day interactions, which always brought us great joy. It was a validation that there was a need for our stories to be shared. The more we wrote, the more thoughtful and aware we became in our professional and personal lives. As a result, we found ourselves trying to dream up ever more creative ways to delight our customers and better handle any stressful situations we encountered, all the while recognizing in each other the skills we were writing about.

"From mindless to mindful" became our guiding principle.

Our experience working together has taught us that these simple truths *are* what make all the difference. From making a great first impression to nurturing a personal connection to giving customers a reason to remember, the customer experience is all about that universal human connection we all share. It doesn't matter if you're a bank executive or a kid at a war wash, these truths are unchanging.

The world may feel like it's spinning a bit faster (and sometimes out of control), and how we conduct business may be galloping forward at a frenetic pace, but the essential element remains: People. Humans! It's a crazy world we live in, this era of high technology and short attention spans. No one has patience for anything or anyone it seems. Information overload contributes to mental fatigue, distraction, and increasing levels of stress at work and at home. People switch to autopilot to cope and enter a state of mindlessness to escape. Fear not. The themes and practical advice in this book are some ways for you to address everyday challenges and calamities. They represent a gentler and kinder approach to rescue one and all from the mindlessness of empty customer experiences and human interactions.

On a personal note, the journey of creating the customer service program and writing this book has been an experience for us like no other. It's our expression of gratitude and appreciation for those who have helped make us a little more mindful in the things we do every day.

We hope our stories will do the same for you too.

Winning Hearts

- Make personal connections with people
- Build anticipation
- Show your appreciation
- Recognize effort and results
- Give people more than they expect
- Leverage strengths
- Practice effective and active listening
- Celebrate successes big and small
- People are going to challenge you—don't forget to have fun
- Smiles and laughter are free—be generous with them

Winning Minds

- Decide what you want to be known for
- Set your goals
- Create a written plan
- Set service standards
- Monitor progress

- Listen to your customers and employees
- Stay loyal to the vision you are creating
- Schedule check-ins and the sharing of ideas
- Observe your team in real time
- Communicate with consistency and clarity

Acknowledgements

Nobody writes a book alone, and we are grateful and appreciative of the passionate individuals who agreed to be featured in this book and allowed us to share their stories and insights. We are particularly grateful to Gary Ford for being a wise mentor and our guide along the way. This has meant the world to us.

Thanks to Insomniac Press for their professionalism and commitment to our book.

We our indebted to our talented and dedicated editor, Dan Varrette, whose unwavering support and guidance are truly appreciated.

A heartfelt thanks to our respective friends and families, who are a constant source of joy and happiness.

Dragica sends thanks to her parents, Mara and Nikola, for their love and support, and to brothers Donny and Michael and their families for always making her smile. To her dear friends Bob and Lucie, Beverley, Wendy, Janey, and Anaid—I am fortunate to have you in my life. And to Amanda D.—Thank you for your encouragement. You inspire me.

Jesse gives thanks to Mike and Joey for picking on

their skinny little brother growing up. Special thanks to Samir, George, Caitlin, Scott, Jordan, CLII, Cooper, and Tanya B. Also thanks to Fernando "Freddy" Frasca, John B., Trevor P., Graham D., and all the hardworking ladies and gents who worked side by side with smiles and laughs at the car wash.

Thanks to our colleagues at Meridian Credit Union, who make it such a great place to work and who always strive to provide a differentiated service experience to our Members—and to each other. Sincere appreciation to those who have directly contributed to the continuation of our personal journeys. (You know who you are.) Special thank you to Cheryl Olsen for being the mediator, always holding the tie-breaking vote and making us smile every day.

Finally, thanks to you, the reader. We hope you enjoyed reading this book as much as we enjoyed writing it.

Endnotes

[1] Carver, R.P., Johnson, R.L., & Friedman, H.L. (1970). Factor analysis of the ability to comprehend time-compressed speech. (Final report for the National Institute for Health). Washington, DC: American Institute for Research.

[2] Taube, Aaron. "Canadian Calls First Doritos Locos Taco One of the Greatest Moments of His Life," *Business Insider*, August 29, 2013: http://www.businessinsider.com/canadian-taco-bell-fans-gladly-eat-their-words-2013-8 (accessed October 5, 2014).

[3] Kansas State University. "What's your name again? Lack of interest, not brain's ability, may be why we forget." ScienceDaily. www.sciencedaily.com/releases/2012/06/120620113027.htm (accessed October 7, 2014).